The Ruqya Handbook

The Ruqya Handbook

A Practical Guide for Spiritual Healing

Abu Nadeer

Alruqya Healing™

The Ruqya Handbook

1st Edition © Alruqya Healing
2021 C.E/1442 A.H

Compiled by Abu Nadeer
ISBN: 9798736443482

Alruqya™
Healing
www.alruqya.co.uk

Published by Alruqya Healing™
7 Sutherland Ave, London W9 2HE
Tel: 07495519354
Email: alruqyahealing@gmail.com
www.alruqya.co.uk

Contents

Acknowledgments

إِنَّ الْحَمْدَ لِلَّهِ نَحْمَدُهُ وَنَسْتَعِينُهُ وَنستغفره ونعوذ بالله من شرور أنفسنا ومن
سيئات أعمالنا مَنْ يَهْدِهِ اللَّهُ فَلَا مُضِلَّ لَهُ وَمَنْ يُضْلِلْ فَلَا هَادِيَ لَهُ وَأَشْهَدُ أَنْ
لَا إِلَهَ إِلَّا اللَّهُ وَحْدَهُ لَا شَرِيكَ لَهُ وَأَنَّ مُحَمَّدًا عَبْدُهُ وَرَسُولُهُ
صلى الله عليه وسلم

All Praise is due to Allah. We praise Him and seek His help and His forgiveness. We seek refuge in Allah, the Most High, from the evil of ourselves and from our wicked deeds. Whoever Allah guides cannot be misguided, and whoever He leads astray, cannot be guided. I testify that there is no true God worthy of being worshipped except Allah, alone, without partner or associate. I further testify that Muhammad is His slave and His Messenger (ﷺ). May Allah's Salaah and Salaam also be granted to the Prophet's pure family and to all of his noble companions.

I would like to thank my family, my friends, and everyone that has helped me and supported me on this journey.

I would like to give a special thanks to my mother who pushed me to learn and study Ruqya. May Allah have mercy on her soul. Ameen.

I would like to give special thanks to my mentor Sheikh Khalid who always called for the correct wellbeing of a person emotionally, spiritually, physically, and mentally. He strives to remove all misconceptions of Ruqya and its improper usage.

In the name of Allah, the Entirely Merciful, the Especially Merciful.

Introduction

This handbook is for those who need help with their affliction, to feel supported and understood. Allah is with you every step of the way in your healing.

No matter what it is you are going through or how it is you are feeling at this very moment, know that you are not alone. Many suffer from spiritual afflictions, though most do not know it or speak about it out of fear of judgement or shame. It is important to not let your life be defined by your spiritual illness.

Take charge of your life and never give up! Keep fighting! All of us have challenges in life. The harder the battle, the sweeter the victory. If you persevere, you will achieve great things!

We as Muslims believe, without a shadow of doubt, that nothing befalls a believer without Allah's permission. There is great wisdom behind all the struggles we go through. When Allah loves a people, He tests them, and that is a way to raise the patient ones higher in status.

Indeed, Allah is preparing us to become strong and firm in our iman. See your affliction as a blessing and as a means of bringing you closer to your Creator.

At some point or another, people begin to struggle in coping with their affliction and tend to become overwhelmed with many different emotions. This is very common, and you should not let yourself become discouraged. You will have some really great days and some really challenging days.

I encourage you to surround yourself with positive people and to be in a positive environment. Thinking and speaking positively will go a long way, along with reading, listening, and watching positive permissible material. It is extremely important to remain positive throughout your healing journey.

Joining a support group with other individuals that are going through similar things or speaking with someone you can confide in is also really beneficial in counteracting your challenges.

I pray to Allah for your affliction to be lifted off of you without any impairments.

Raqi Abu Nadeer

Preface

I was inspired to write this handbook due to the shortage of information on the subject of Ruqya and its correct method in the English language. Being a Raqi for over 20 years, I felt the need to compile this Ruqya handbook in hopes that it will benefit the ummah by the will of Allah while trying to keep to the most authentic hadiths and understanding of the pious predecessors.

Through this handbook, I hope to clear up the misconceptions of Ruqya, to highlight Ruqya performed according to the Qur'an and Sunnah, to raise awareness of improper Ruqya and of misleading practitioners, and to help those that are afflicted heal according to the Qur'an and Sunnah.

We ask Allah to bring goodness to this handbook and to put blessings in it for all. May He grant us the correct knowledge in which we can help all those that are afflicted.

Note to the Reader

1. *Acknowledge:* The first step to recovery is acknowledgement. Before you can fix your problem, you need to first identify it. From picking up this handbook, it is already shown you have acknowledged the problem. Next, you need to know that in order to deal effectively with your affliction, you need to have emotional control and take preventative measures with a positive mindset. Know that nothing happens unless it is decreed by Allah, so think well of Allah at all times and in all circumstances. Put your trust in Him and focus on the bigger picture which is the Hereafter and *"That is the great success (Paradise)…"* [Interpretation of Surah Al-Maa'idah 5:119].

And Allah Says:

تِلْكَ ٱلدَّارُ ٱلْءَاخِرَةُ نَجْعَلُهَا لِلَّذِينَ لَا يُرِيدُونَ عُلُوًّا فِى ٱلْأَرْضِ وَلَا فَسَادًا ۚ وَٱلْعَٰقِبَةُ لِلْمُتَّقِينَ

"That home of the Hereafter We assign to those who do not desire exaltedness upon the earth or corruption. And the [best] outcome is for the righteous" [Interpretation of Surah Al-Qasas 28:83].

By striving to achieve righteousness and closeness to Allah, and His remembrance, and all of the above mentioned, it is like arming yourself with the right mental and spiritual strategies to help you make a successful breakthrough in unblocking your affliction.

2. *Be Optimistic:* Our circumstances will always vary, and it is important to have an optimistic outlook in life. Shaytan wants to cause you grief, stress, anxiety, and hopelessness to divert you from the right path. You can put an end to this by not feeding into negativity and by focusing on the good things in your life. Always look at the bright side and know the reward is great for the patient one, and *"Verily, Allah is with the patient"* [Interpretation of Surah Al-Baqarah 2:153].

3. *Accept Allah's Decree:* One of the biggest benefits of believing in the Divine Decree is that all of our affairs and power are in His Hands. There is great wisdom behind whatever Allah has decreed for us. Knowing this will relieve you from your day to day worries and stresses associated with your affliction that is impacting your life. *"Allah (Alone) is sufficient for us, and He is The Best Disposer of affairs (for us)"* [Interpretation of Surah Al-Imran 3:173].

4. *Have Tawakkul in Allah:* Rely on Allah in all aspects of your life, by taking the correct means and measures, to overcome obstacles in life. *"And rely upon Allah; and sufficient is Allah as Disposer of affairs"* [Interpretation of Surah Al-Ahzab 33:3]. Taking the correct means and measures does not contradict reliance in Allah and putting your trust in Him.

5. *Be Mindful of Allah & He Will Protect You:* Ensure that you are fulfilling all the obligatory acts of Islam, which are the pillars of your Deen. Strive to perfect your five daily prayers, do your adhkar, recite Qur'an and understand its commands to ward

off harm as it is a protection against evil and a cure for illness of the heart, body and mind.

6. *Du'a:* Allah has promised you that He will respond to all those that call upon Him. *"Call upon Me; I will respond to you"* [Interpretation of Surah Al-Ghafir 40:60].

Allah responds even to the disbeliever when he calls upon Him in desperation, *"And when harm touches you upon the sea, those that you call upon besides Him vanish from you except Him (Allah Alone). But when He brings you safely to land, you turn away (from Him). And man is ever ungrateful"* [Interpretation of Surah Al-Isra' 17:67]. When Allah answers their Du'a and saves them, they forget and become arrogant and turn back in disbelief.

The Prophet (ﷺ) said: "Fear the prayer of the oppressed, even if he is a disbeliever, for there is no barrier between it and Allah."[1]

If Allah answers the Du'a of a disbeliever, would He not then answer the Du'a of a believer?

7. *The Cure:* Know that Allah is The One who heals whoever He wills, and He Alone decrees the cure. *"And when I am ill, it is He who cures me"* [Interpretation of Surah Ash-Shu'ara 26:80].

Abu Hurayrah (may Allah be pleased with him) said: The Prophet (ﷺ) said, "Allah has not brought down an illness, except He accompanied with it a cure."[2]

In Ahmad, similar to the above, "Those who have knowledge of it, have knowledge of it, and those who are ignorant of it, are ignorant of it."

---

[1] Reported by Ahmad
[2] Reported by Bukhari

Please continue to have patience. May Allah give you strength and healing.

Chapter 1

The Enmity of Iblees

Shaytan – An Avowed Enemy to Mankind

Remember, you have an arch enemy that does not want you to succeed. Allah has informed us in the Qur'an about the enmity of Iblees towards man and has warned us of the plots and plans of Shaytan and his troops, whose sole objective is to misguide man and to encourage mankind upon evil.

كَمَثَلِ الشَّيْطَانِ إِذْ قَالَ لِلْإِنسَانِ اكْفُرْ فَلَمَّا كَفَرَ قَالَ إِنِّي بَرِيءٌ مِّنكَ إِنِّي أَخَافُ اللَّهَ رَبَّ الْعَالَمِينَ

"[The hypocrites are] like the example of Satan when he says to man, 'Disbelieve.' But when he disbelieves, he (Satan) says, 'Indeed, I am disassociated from you. Indeed, I fear Allah, Lord of the worlds'"
[Interpretation of Surah Al-Hashr 59:16].

He does not just whisper to man and fill his heart with doubt in his faith, but he also can attack one physically and spiritually. Shaytan would use the evil eye and envy, teach

1

magic to man, and even possess man to lead him astray and towards hellfire.

وَإِذْ زَيَّنَ لَهُمُ ٱلشَّيْطَٰنُ أَعْمَٰلَهُمْ وَقَالَ لَا غَالِبَ لَكُمُ ٱلْيَوْمَ مِنَ ٱلنَّاسِ وَإِنِّى جَارٌ لَّكُمْ ۖ فَلَمَّا تَرَآءَتِ ٱلْفِئَتَانِ نَكَصَ عَلَىٰ عَقِبَيْهِ وَقَالَ إِنِّى بَرِىٓءٌ مِّنكُمْ إِنِّىٓ أَرَىٰ مَا لَا تَرَوْنَ إِنِّىٓ أَخَافُ ٱللَّهَ ۚ وَٱللَّهُ شَدِيدُ ٱلْعِقَابِ

"And [remember] when Satan made their deeds pleasing to them and said, 'No one can overcome you today from among the people, and indeed, I am your protector.' But when the two armies sighted each other, he turned on his heels and said, 'Indeed, I am disassociated from you. Indeed, I see what you do not see; indeed, I fear Allah. And Allah is severe in penalty" [Interpretation of Surah Al-Anfal 8:48].

وَأَعِدُّوا۟ لَهُم مَّا ٱسْتَطَعْتُم مِّن قُوَّةٍ وَمِن رِّبَاطِ ٱلْخَيْلِ تُرْهِبُونَ بِهِۦ عَدُوَّ ٱللَّهِ وَعَدُوَّكُمْ وَءَاخَرِينَ مِن دُونِهِمْ لَا تَعْلَمُونَهُمُ ٱللَّهُ يَعْلَمُهُمْ ۚ وَمَا تُنفِقُوا۟ مِن شَىْءٍ فِى سَبِيلِ ٱللَّهِ يُوَفَّ إِلَيْكُمْ وَأَنتُمْ لَا تُظْلَمُونَ

"And prepare against them whatever you are able of power and of steeds of war by which you may terrify the enemy of Allah and your enemy and others besides them whom you do not know[3] [but] whom Allah knows. And whatever you spend in the cause of Allah will be fully repaid to you, and you will not be wronged" [Interpretation of Surah Al-Anfal 8:60].

In hadith, Jabir reported that Allah's Messenger (ﷺ) said: Iblis places his throne upon water; he then sends detachments (for creating dissension); the nearer to him in rank are those who

---

[3] Others besides them whom you do not know are the Jinn, Ibn Kathir.

2

are most notorious in creating dissension. One of them comes and says: "I did so and so." And Iblees says: "You have done nothing." Then one amongst them comes and says: I did not spare so and so until I sowed the seed of discord between a husband and a wife." The Satan goes near him and says: "You have done well." A'mash said: He then embraces him.[4]

When you ponder upon these verses and others like it in the Book of Allah and the Sunnah, you come to the conclusion a believer is like a warrior in a battle with Shaytan. Shaytan is the number one enemy towards man who does not cease fighting. There is no escaping it except facing it, and resisting it in the way of Allah.

---

[4] Reported by Muslim

Chapter 2

Tawheed

'Aqeedah[5] is the core of Islam. Tawheed,[6] the oneness of Allah, is the foundation of this Ruqya handbook. It is the first and most important aspect that we must focus on and set straight in order to be successful in general terms, but also in relation to the devils and spiritual afflictions, for the belief in Tawheed (monotheism) is the purpose for which Allah created both mankind and Jinn (spirits made from smokeless fire).

Allah Says:

$$وَمَا خَلَقْتُ الْجِنَّ وَالْإِنسَ إِلَّا لِيَعْبُدُونِ$$

"And I created not the Jinn and mankind except that they should worship Me (Alone)" [Interpretation of Surah Ad-Dhariyat 51:56].

---

[5] In Islam, 'aqeedah refers to the matters which are known from the Qur'an and sound ahadeeth, and which the Muslim must believe in his heart, in acknowledgement of the truth of Allah and His Messenger.

[6] Shar'i definition of Tawheed means believing in Allah alone as God and Lord and attributing to Him alone all the attributes of Lordship and divinity. It may be defined as follows: Believing that Allah is One with no partner or associate in His Lordship (Ruboobiyyah), Divinity (Uloohiyyah), or names and attributes (Al-asma' wa-sifaat).

4

The Prophet Muhammad (ﷺ) was sent to take people out from the darkness and bring them into the light. He established the message of Tawheed (the oneness of God) and removed the flames of Shirk[7] (associating partners with Allah and ascribing God's attributes to others than Him).

This is why one of the most important obligations is to know the meaning of shirk, its seriousness, and its different types, so that our Tawheed and our Islam may be complete, so one can distinguish between right and wrong, and so our faith may be sound.

Therefore, it is essential to understand that Tawheed is the solution. It is what gives the believer strength and protection. It is what expels the hardships of this world, and it is what grants contentment, relief and victory.

Ibn Qayyim al-Jawzeeyah (رحمه الله) said:

> There is nothing that drives away the afflictions of this world except Tawheed. That is why the supplication of the distressed person is with Tawheed. Such as the supplication of Yunus (Jonah)[8] (عليه السلام). The distressed person does not supplicate with what Yunus (Jonah) (عليه السلام) supplicated with except that Allah releases him from his hardship because of Tawheed. There is nothing more gruesome than Shirk, and there is nothing that can rescue you from it except Tawheed. It is the refuge for creation, its shelter, its fortress, and its aid [Al-Fawa'id].

Unfortunately, many Muslims have neglected Ruqya and its concepts. Some may have never even thought about it and others may even look at it as nonsense. However, the true

---

[7] In Sharee'ah, Shirk means ascribing a partner or rival to Allah in Lordship (Ruboobiyyah), worship or in His Names and Attributes.

[8] *Supplication of Yunus* (عليه السلام):
لا إله إلا أنت سبحانك إني كنت من الظالمين

believer sees the benefit of Ruqya healing for all types of sicknesses, including physical, spiritual and psychological illnesses too. For indeed the Book of Allah confirms this: the permissibility of seeking healing through Qur'anic recitation and the Prophet's (ﷺ) established prayers.

Allah Says:

$$قُلْ هُوَ لِلَّذِينَ ءَامَنُوا۟ هُدًى وَشِفَآءٌ$$

"… *Say, it is, for those who believe, a guidance and cure…*"
[Interpretation of Surah Al-Fussilat 41:44].

And Allah Says:

$$وَنُنَزِّلُ مِنَ ٱلْقُرْءَانِ مَا هُوَ شِفَآءٌ وَرَحْمَةٌ لِّلْمُؤْمِنِينَ$$

"*And We send down from the Qur'an that which is a healing and a mercy to those who believe…*" [Interpretation of Surah Al-Isra'
17:82].

Through these verses Allah informs us again and again that the Qur'an is a healing and a cure which is why we find many reports mentioning the practice of Ruqya during the life of the Prophet (ﷺ).

One particular narration that stands out and signifies the importance and benefits of Ruqya is of Angel Jibreel (عليه السلام), the best of all angels, who came down and performed Ruqya upon the Prophet (ﷺ) when the Prophet complained of an illness:

> Abu Sa'eed reported that Jibreel came to Allah's Messenger (ﷺ) and said, "O Muhammad, have you fallen ill?" Thereupon

6

he said: "Yes." Jibreel said: "In the name of Allah, I perform Ruqya on you, from everything that would harm you, and from the evil of every person or envious eye, may Allah cure you. In the name of Allah, I perform Ruqya on you."[9]

The best of creations and the most beloved and closest to Allah, utilised Ruqya so how can we ignore and neglect this effective method of healing today?

The above narration is just one account, but there are many more accounts reported of the Prophet (ﷺ) and his companions, advising others to seek Ruqya and performing it upon themselves and others, which will be covered in this handbook.

For example, The Messenger (ﷺ) even advised his wife Aisha (may Allah be pleased with her) to seek Ruqya.

Narrated from A'isha (may Allah be pleased with her), said the Messenger of Allah (ﷺ) used to tell me to seek Ruqya for the evil eye.[10]

So, my brothers and sisters, implement Ruqya upon yourselves and your families and reap the benefits by the permission of Allah and get closer to Him.

---

[9] Reported by Muslim
[10] Reported by Bukhari and Muslim

Chapter 3

The Importance of Prayer

You might be a practicing Muslim or not, maybe you are not a Muslim or do not follow a certain religion, but as long as you call upon Him, the One Deity, the One who created the heavens and the Earth and He who is the only one worthy of worship, He will answer your call. All the Prophets and Messengers including Noah, Abraham, Moses, Jesus, and the seal of the prophets, Muhammad (ﷺ), called and worshipped the One God that has no imperfections or human attributes, Allah—there is nothing like Him.

In Islam, the most important thing is the five daily prayers. The prayers are one of the five pillars of faith as they establish a relationship with our Creator. They are a commandment that must be fulfilled by all Muslims.

In a hadith, Abu Hurayrah reported that the Prophet (ﷺ) said:

> The first action for which a servant of Allah will be held accountable on the Day of Resurrection will be his prayers. If they are in order, he will have prospered and succeeded. If they are lacking, he will have failed and lost. If there is something defective in his obligatory prayers, then the Almighty Lord will

say: See if my servant has any voluntary prayers that can complete what is insufficient in his obligatory prayers. The rest of his deeds will be judged the same way [Sunan al-Tirmidhi].

The overall effect that the prayers should have upon humans is described in the Qur'an: *"Indeed, mankind was created anxious: when evil touches him, he is impatient, and when good touches him, he withholds it, except the observers of prayer, those who are constant in their prayer..."* [Interpretation of Surah Al-Ma'arij 19-23].

From my experience, most individuals suffering from affliction are those that have not established their five daily prayers. Once they start praying, there is a noticeable improvement in their condition.

As for the hereafter, Allah's forgiveness and pleasure are closely related to one's prayers: *"Certainly will the believers have succeeded. They who are during their prayer humbly intent"* [Interpretation of Surah Al-Mu'minun 23:1-2].

Successful is the one who attains peace and tranquility in his prayer and is constantly trying to achieve it, forgetting all the worries of this life whilst standing before Allah, having fear and hope in Him, with total tranquility, not looking left or right, but where he places his forehead, humbling his body, mind, and soul.

A hadith narrated by Salman ibn Jadah: The Prophet said (ﷺ), "O Bilal, call to the prayer, for the prayer gives us comfort."[11]

The prayer was the most beloved act of worship to the Prophet (ﷺ), feeling comfort in the prayer, entering it, focusing on it, with no distraction of the worldly affairs and its problems. What comes with this is the closeness to Allah, peace

---

[11] Reported by Abu Dawud, authenticated by Albanee

to the soul, and tranquility of the heart. It is not surprising to find comfort in the prayer, for the one who loves it experiences peace and tranquility in that moment. For those who do not experience this,

Allah Says:

وَإِنَّهَا لَكَبِيرَةٌ إِلَّا عَلَى ٱلْخَٰشِعِينَ

"...and indeed, it is difficult except for the humbly submissive (to Allah in the prayer)" [Interpretation of Surah Al-Baqarah 2:45].

As for those who do not pray in this life, there will be a painful torment: *"(And asking them), 'What put you in Saqar (Hell)? They will say, 'We were not of those who prayed'"* [Surah Interpretation of Al-Muddaththir 74:42-43].

When calamities hit, surprisingly many individuals will turn to everything else except their prayer. They will turn towards others seeking comfort and counseling. They will seek different types of therapy in hopes of a solution and will turn towards many pagan practices and towards the likes of spiritual meditation while neglecting their prayer.

You will find people turn to everything else and turn away from their prayer. These verses show the importance of prayer and how one's prayers should not be neglected. One should strive to perfect it as with Allah lies your success.

In a hadith, Abu Hurayrah reported that the Prophet (ﷺ) said:

> When a bondsman, a Muslim or a believer washes his face (in course of ablution), every sin he contemplated with his eyes will be washed away from his face along with water, or with the last drop of water; when he washes his hands, every sin they

10

wrought will be effaced from his hands with the water, or with the last drop of water; and when he washes his feet, every sin towards which his feet have walked will be washed away with the water or with the last drop of water with the result that he comes out pure from all sins.[12]

Good deeds that erase sin include wudu, the five daily prayers, and Hajj and 'Umrah. The greatest of good deeds is Tawheed (affirmation of the Oneness of Allah), and the gravest of evil deeds is Kufr (disbelief) and Shirk (ascribing partners to Allah).

---

[12] Reported by Muslim

Chapter 4

Seeking Treatment in Islam

The Qur'an is a Shifa[13] which encompasses everything: the heart, the mind and the soul. It takes away doubts, ignorance and evil thoughts, and is a cure for the body from all pain and sickness. Allah also mentions, *"Say, 'It is, for those who believe, a guidance and cure'"* [Interpretation of Surah Al-Fussilat 41:44].

If one was to ponder upon the Qur'an and Sunnah, one would find many examples of protecting the body and soul from harm such as the rituals of wudu, ghusl, salah, fasting, and hajj. If one was to ponder upon these acts mentioned, they are to preserve the body and soul. Likewise, some of the acts Allah has prohibited include drinking alcohol, eating pork, gambling, and committing adultery because it is harmful to the body and soul.

Allah says in the Qur'an,

---

[13] Shifa in Arabic means cure or healing.

$$وَنُنَزِّلُ مِنَ ٱلْقُرْءَانِ مَا هُوَ شِفَآءٌ وَرَحْمَةٌ لِّلْمُؤْمِنِينَ ۙ وَلَا يَزِيدُ ٱلظَّٰلِمِينَ إِلَّا خَسَارًا$$

"And We send down of the Qur'an that which is a healing and a mercy for the believers, but it does not increase the wrongdoers except in loss"
[Interpretation of Surah Al-Isra' 17:82].

In the Qur'an, Allah speaks about honey as one cure which is a tangible substance:

$$يَخْرُجُ مِنْ بُطُونِهَا شَرَابٌ مُّخْتَلِفٌ أَلْوَٰنُهُ فِيهِ شِفَآءٌ لِّلنَّاسِ ۗ إِنَّ فِى ذَٰلِكَ لَءَايَةً لِّقَوْمٍ يَتَفَكَّرُونَ$$

"There comes forth from their bellies, a drink of varying colour wherein is healing for men. Verily, in this is indeed a sign for people who think"
[Interpretation of the Surah Al-Nahl 16:69].

Allah has spoken about different illnesses and problems people encounter in their life in the Qur'an. He has indicated solutions to their problems in many places in the Qur'an and Sunnah.

Ibn Qayyim says:

> Allah mentions the person who is sick in the time of hajj and fasting and performing ablution to make it easy on the person and shows you the greatness of the Qur'an and you will find the principles of medicine are of three: preserving health, protecting from disease or harm, and extracting the harm or disease.[14]

---

14 Zaad Al Ma'ad

13

Allah also mentions the blind, the limp, and the ill in the Qur'an and likewise He has mentioned the word *cure*.

The Qur'an has a cure for every problem as Allah says, *"We have neglected nothing in the Book"* [Interpretation of Surah Al-Anam 6:38]. There is a solution or an indication of a solution for every situation one might face in life.

The Prophet Muhammad (ﷺ) said to seek treatment for indeed Allah has not placed a sickness except he has placed for it a cure, a cure for everything except for the sickness of old age.[15]

Abu'l-Darda' (may Allah be pleased with him) said: The Messenger of Allah (ﷺ) said, "Allah has sent down the disease and the cure, and has made for every illness the cure. So treat sickness, but do not use anything haram."[16]

Ibn Qayyim (may Allah have mercy on him) said:

> In the statement of the Prophet (ﷺ), "for every illness there is a cure" is a glad tiding to the patient as well as the doctor as it acts as an encouragement in finding and discovering that particular cure and in this the patient feels a sense of ease and hope that there is a cure for their disease, hence the heat of their despair cools down, the door of hope becomes wide open and whenever their soul becomes stronger it brings back to life the warmth of its instincts which then is a reason in strengthening the life of the living creatures, plants and natural organisms. Whenever these lives are strengthened it strengthens the immunity that the organism holds therefore overcoming and expelling the sickness from the body. Likewise, if the doctor knew that to this illness there is a cure they should seek for it, and just as the body faces varying degrees of illnesses the heart also faces illnesses of varying degrees and there is no illness for the heart except that Allah

---

[15] Reported by Abu Dawud and Tirmidhi, authenticated by Albanee
[16] Reported by Abu Dawud

made a cure for it, so if the individual knew of the medicine (related to the disease of the heart) then they should use it, and if it happened to encounter the disease then he (the ill person) will be cured with the will of Allah."[17]

Ultimately, our objective is to seek medical treatment in the Words of Allah, Prophetic Supplications and through the prescriptions of Allah and His Messenger from the Book (of Allah) and the Sunnah.

Islam encourages us to protect our well-being and to seek treatment for our ailments. The only condition is that it must be permissible. Verily, Allah has brought down the disease and its cure. And He made for every disease, a cure. So, treat yourselves and do not treat yourself with impermissible means.[18] In another hadith, the Prophet has prohibited medicine that is impure.[19] It is not permissible for a Muslim to seek medicine or healing that comes from prohibited or impure sources whether physical or spiritual as indeed, Allah has not placed your cure in what He has forbidden for you.[20]

It should be noted that Ruqya is one of the types of remedy prescribed in Islam, but there are certain conditions for it to be beneficial and permissible, just as physical medicine has conditions for it to be suitable for a Muslim individual.

Additionally, people may search for alternative healing methods. There is nothing wrong with this as long as it falls under the teachings and principles of Islam. However, unfortunately there is an increase of many individuals turning to alternative healing methods such as crystal healing, reiki healing, energy healing, and the like. Even witchcraft,

---

[17] Zaad Al Ma'ad

[18] Explanation of Sunan Abu Dawud, Awn al-Abood

[19] Reported by Imam Ahmad, authenticated by Albanee

[20] Reported by Imam Ahmad, authenticated by Albanee

especially in the West, has become a trend amongst the youth. This does not come as a surprise because they have been exposed and nurtured through cartoons, films, and shows which glorify witchcraft. These types of methods have become a trend as increasingly celebrities have been sharing their photos and experiences on social media for their followers to see. For example, one can find many celebrities wearing crystal necklaces as fashion with the poisoned thinking that the crystals are a form of protection and healing. Also, you will notice an increase of individuals wearing charm bracelets as a fashion trend. Charms and amulets go back to paganism worship similar to Christians wearing the cross around their necks.

With the lack of knowledge of Tawheed, one can fall into great error which can lead them out of the fold of Islam. The same danger can be said to those that seek help from individuals such as clairvoyants and mediums who claim to communicate with the unseen or who claim to possess the power of miracles.

Chapter 5

What is Ruqya?

The Definition of Ruqya

Ruqya in the Arabic language comes from the word 'Ouda (عود), which means turning to or seeking refuge in.[21] For the one who is afflicted turns to Ruqya so he can be healed. This is the linguistic understanding of Ruqya regardless of it being permissible or impermissible. It is applied to people who suffer from fits, fevers and other ailments. In the English language, it is usually referred to as spells, charms, incantations, and so on.

The scholars refer to Ruqya as 'Ouda which is treated with supplications and seeking the cure.[22]

Shaykh Ibn Taymiyyah said in Majmoo' al-Fataawa: "Ruqya means seeking refuge and Al-Istirqaa (asking for Ruqya), and it is a type of supplication."

---

[21] Qamoos Al-Muheet
[22] Shams ul-Haqq, explanation of Sunan Abu Dawud, Awn al-Abood

The History of Ruqya

Ruqya has been practiced throughout history and even before Islam. People from the past would turn to Ruqya and believed they would benefit from it in it of itself in order to fight spiritual afflictions as many faced spiritual afflictions. Ruqya is old as ancient times.

Unfortunately, throughout the centuries, many groups of people were deceived and misguided in the matter of Ruqya. The Shayateen of man and Jinn played a major role in this.

Instead, people resorted to looking to the stars, worshipping them and the Jinn. They would use spells, stones, jewels, and other charms for healing with the guidance of soothsayers and magicians, eventually turning the masses to worship other than Allah. They believed in the magic, became misguided and in turn misguided others.

Islam came to abolish all misconceptions of Ruqya, and to establish its correct understanding and methodology.

Islamic Technical Term of Ruqya

In Islam, Ruqya is the recitation of Qur'an, Allah's Perfect names and attributes, prophetic supplications and supplications that are free from Shirk, and with the belief that Ruqya has no effect in it of itself, but rather, it is only effective by the permission of Allah.

Unfortunately, some Muslims of today have neglected performing Ruqya. They have turned to magicians some of which who may claim to perform Ruqya but are far from it. Some Muslims also have turned to fortune-tellers and spiritual healers who claim to have knowledge of the unseen or to possess the ability to perform miracles. Ruqya may seem as

18

senseless to some and others will only link it to spiritual afflictions such as Jinn possession, evil eye, or black magic. However, that is not the case, as Ruqya has a very positive impact on illnesses that conventional doctors cannot understand with many eye witnessing accounts. It is a Sunnah and was performed by many of the pious predecessors for physical and non-physical illnesses and has been recorded in their books.

It is important to distinguish Ruqya according to Islamic teachings: Ruqya Shariah (Lawful Ruqya) and Ruqya Shirkiyah (Unlawful Ruqya).

Chapter 6

The Use of Ruqya

Ruqya is one of the greatest remedies that a believer should use regularly. Treating illnesses by the means of the Qur'an and Sunnah is something that has become forgotten. Ruqya as prescribed in the Shariah is for every illness whether physical, psychological or spiritual.

As mentioned earlier, people of different cultures and religions use various forms of Ruqya, most of which contain Sihr (magic), Shirk, senseless words, etc. This is why the Prophet (صلى الله عليه وسلم) prohibited the use of Ruqya at first:

Ibn Mas'ud (رضي الله عنه) reported: The Prophet (صلى الله عليه وسلم) said, "Indeed, spells (Ruqya), amulets and Tiwala (love-charms) are all acts of Shirk."[23]

Whoever is affected by Sihr should not treat it with Sihr, because evil cannot be removed by evil, and Kufr cannot be removed by Kufr. Hence, when the Prophet (صلى الله عليه وسلم) was asked

---

[23] Reported by Abu Dawud, authenticated by Albanee

about An-Nushrah[24] (treating Sihr with Sihr), he said, "This is the work of the Shaytaan."[25]

Nushrah means removing Sihr from a person who has been affected by it by using additional Sihr. However, if it is treated by means of the Qur'an and permissible medicines or Ruqya prescribed in Islam, there is nothing wrong with that. Treating Sihr with Sihr is not permitted, because it includes worshipping the Shayateen (devils) and doing a lot of Shirk and Kufr.

Later on, the Prophet (ﷺ) permitted the use of Ruqya that was free from Shirk.

---

[24] There are two types of Nushrah. One that is prohibited and one that is not.

[25] Reported by Ahmad, authenticated by Albanee

Chapter 7

The Conditions of Permissible Ruqya

There are two types of Ruqya: Ruqya Shirkiyya (impermissible Ruqya) and Ruqya Shari'ah (permissible Ruqya).

Ruqya Shari'ah (Islamic Ruqya)

- It calls to Tawheed and to the correct 'Aqeedah.
- It calls to practicing the Deen[26] in the correct manner.
- It helps with a person's spiritual journey.
- It revives the Prophetic Tradition (Sunnah).
- It brings one closer to Allah and makes him rely upon Him alone.
- It is classified as remembrance of Allah.
- It is a successful treatment for grief, sorrow, anxiety, Jinn possession, evil eye, and magic.
- It helps an individual stay close to the Qur'an.
- It cuts the pathway to soothsayers, séances, mediums and magicians who falsely claim to have knowledge of the unseen.

---

[26] Deen means way of life/religion.

- It is an act of worship and a means to strengthen your iman (faith).
- It prevents one from falling into the shirk of believing a Raqi has the cure. It stops one's heart from becoming attached to the people and encourages one to seek the cure in Allah alone.
- It enables one to have a stronger relationship with Allah.

Al-Haafiz Ibn Hajar (may Allah have mercy on him) said:

> The scholars unanimously agreed that it is permissible to use Ruqya if three conditions are met: it should be based on the words of Allah, may He be glorified and exalted, or His names or His attributes; it should be in Arabic or in words the meaning of which can be understood; and it should be accepted that Ruqya does not have any effect in and of itself, rather that happens by the will and decree of Allah.

Conditions of Permissible Ruqya:

- *Must be with Allah's words, names and attributes:* In a hadith recorded by Muslim, the Prophet (ﷺ) said, "There is nothing wrong with Ruqya that does not involve shirk."

- *Must be with words that are understood:* If the words are not understood, then it can consist of words of magic and we find many Taweez contain unknown words and symbols that are not understood.

- *Must be believed that Allah alone is the true healer:* The true believers believe that the only cure comes from Allah and if they were to become ill then Allah alone would cure them. Allah says, *"So seek refuge in Allah. Indeed, He alone is the All-Hearing, All-Seeing"* [Interpretation of Surah Al-Ghafir 40:56]. Neither the person seeking

Ruqya, nor the person doing the Ruqya can believe that the Ruqya itself has an independent power of cure or protection. They must both put their full trust in Allah, relying fully on Him and believing that the Ruqya is a means that Allah has created for them.

Is Ruqya restricted to what is reported in the Qur'an and Sunnah?

The scholars have two different opinions, and both hold to their evidences. As for those who say it is not restricted, it must meet certain conditions because of the hadith of Jabir in Sahih Muslim: "He who amongst you is competent to do good to his brother should do that."

In another hadith by Awf ibn Malik in Sahih Muslim, it states that "there is nothing wrong with a Ruqya that does not involve Shirk." Also, in a hadith of Abu Sa'id Al-Khudri in Sahih Bukhari the Prophet (ﷺ) said, "How do you know that Surah Al-Fatiha is a Ruqya?"

Is Ruqya restricted to a certain illness?

From a hadith in Muslim: Jibril said, "In the name of Allah, I perform Ruqya for you from everything that is harming you."

This is one of the many hadiths which highlight that Ruqya can be performed on any element that is harming a person. One can even combine their conventional treatment with Ruqya.

In conclusion, Islamic Ruqya is Ruqya that uses permissible and prophetic supplications, good words that are free from shirk, and the permissible practices of our predecessors.

Every good word has an effect upon the evil eye, Jinn and magic. Additionally, the tested methods of treatment that are also free from shirk are also beneficial by the will of Allah The Most High.

Chapter 8

The Practices of Impermissible Ruqya

Ruqya Shirkiyyah (Pagan Ruqya)

- It calls upon other than Allah.
- It calls towards innovations, myths and superstition.
- It turns the heart away from Allah.
- It encourages soothsayers, magicians and charlatans.
- It is an act of evil worship whereby sacrificing animals and human beings etc.
- It weakens the person's faith and darkens the heart.
- It leads to all evil and immoral acts.
- It leads to the loss of this world and the loss of the hereafter.

Impermissible Ruqya

- *Consists of Shirk:* In a hadith recorded by Abu Dawood, authenticated by Albanee: "Indeed incorrect Ruqya, amulets and Tiwalahs all manifest shirk."

- *Contains magic:* In a hadith, Jaber reported: Prophet Muhammad (ﷺ) said, "Nushrah is from the doings of shaytaan."[27] The meaning of Nushrah in this hadith is a magic spell done to counter another magic spell. In English, this is known as white magic.

- *Is sought from magicians or soothsayers:* In a hadith, Abu Hurayah reported: The Prophet (ﷺ) said, "Whomever goes to a soothsayer or fortune teller and believes in what he says has indeed rejected what has been revealed to Prophet Muhammad (ﷺ)."[28] Also, the Prophet Muhammad (ﷺ) said, "Whomever goes to a soothsayer or fortune teller and believes in what he says has indeed rejected what has been revealed to Prophet Muhammad (ﷺ)."[29] In another hadith, Abu Hurayah reported: The Prophet (ﷺ) said, "Whomever goes to a soothsayer and believes what he tells him, or performs intercourse with a menstrual woman, or performs intercourse with a woman in her anus, has surely disbelieved what has been revealed to Muhammad (ﷺ)."[30] In another hadith, The Prophet (ﷺ) said, "Whomever goes to a fortune teller and asks him for something from the unseen, then his prayer will not be accepted for 40 nights."[31]

- *Is applied under bizarre conditions or makes bizarre claims:* For example, claiming to catch or imprison a Jinni, having the person do Ruqya in the dark or telling the person to look into the water or fire while doing Ruqya. These

---

[27] Reported by Ahmad, authenticated by Albanee

[28] Reported by Imam Ahmad

[29] Reported by Ahmad, Al-Hakim, authenticated Albanee

[30] Reported by At-Tirmidi

[31] Reported by Muslim and Ahmad

27

are just a few examples of many of the misguided methods.

- *Consists of amulets and talismans:* The Prophet of Allah (ﷺ) said, "Whoever hangs up an amulet is guilty of Shirk."[32]

- *Consists of charms and symbols:* For example, blue beads, horseshoes, rabbit's foot, leaves or plants, seashells, blackseed seeds, onions, salt, pagan charms, the hand of Fatima, wind catchers, dream catchers etc.

Any form of charm or symbol is prohibited if it is believed to have a form of protection or cure such as the growing popularity of healing crystals. Using them is a serious act of Shirk.

Ibn Ma'sud reported when he saw a tied string on his wife's neck for Ruqya (protection) he cut it off her neck and said, "Indeed members of Ibn Ma'sud's family are in no need of joining partners with Allah," which He did not permit. "Truly I heard Allah's messenger (ﷺ) say, 'Indeed incorrect Ruqya, amulets and tiwalahs all manifest shirk.'"[33]

In another hadith the Prophet (ﷺ) said, "Anyone who hangs something for protection will be yielded to that thing."[34]

---

[32] Reported by Ahmad

[33] Reported by Abu Dawood, authenticated by Albanee

[34] Reported by Abu Dawood and Tirmidhi, verified to be Hassan by Albanee

Unfortunately, many people including Muslims are engaging in these practices without knowing its pagan origins and the consequences of such evil acts. Islam came to wipe away falsehood and bring forth truth and light.

Chapter 9

The Implementation of Permissible Ruqya

Ruqya Can Be Performed on A Physical Ailment

In a hadith, Jabir reported: Allah's Messenger (ﷺ) prohibited incantation. Then the people of Amr bin Hazm came to Allah's Messenger (ﷺ) and said, "We know an incantation which we use for curing the sting of the scorpion, but you have prohibited it." They recited (the words of incantation) before him, whereupon he said, "I do not see any harm (in it), so he who amongst you is competent to do good to his brother should do that."[35]

From this hadith, we understand:
- Ruqya was performed before Islam; and of its types, the permissible and impermissible which is why the Prophet (ﷺ) disapproved it at first.

---

[35] Reported by Muslim

- After the Prophet (ﷺ) inspected it, he approved of it and then legalized it.
- It was used as a treatment for a scorpion sting. This shows that Ruqya can be used for physical and external ailments and for any venomous bites.
- Whoever is able to perform Ruqya, he is encouraged to do so.
- Ruqya is allowed as long as it does not consist of any forms of Shirk and does not go against Islamic principles.

In a hadith, Ali (may Allah be pleased with him) reported: A scorpion bit the Prophet (ﷺ) while he was praying. When he finished, he said "May the curse of Allah be upon the scorpion. It does not leave alone the one who is praying or anyone else." Then he (ﷺ) asked for water and salt. Thereupon, he (ﷺ) started to wipe the sting and read Surah Al-Kafirun, Surah Al-Falaq, and Surah An-Nas.[36]

From this hadith, we understand:
- One can use water and salt combined with the recitation of Qur'an.
- Any pure liquids and herbs can be used for Ruqya purposes such as those mentioned in the Qur'an and Sunnah as well as those not mentioned but have a healing effect.

Performing Ruqya On Oneself and Others

Narrated by 'Uthmaan ibn Abi'l-'Aas that he complained to the Messenger of Allah (ﷺ) about a pain in his body that he had suffered from the time he became Muslim. The Messenger of Allah (ﷺ) said to him, "Put your hand on the part of the

---

[36] Reported by Tabarani, authenticated by Albanee

body that hurts and say Bismillah (باسم الله ، ثلاثاً) (in the name of Allah) three times. And say seven times:

$$وقل : سبع مرات : أعوذ بالله وقدرته من شر ما أجد وأحاذر$$

A'oodhu Billaahi wa qudratihi min sharri ma ajid wa uhaadhir (I seek refuge in Allah and His power from the evil of what I feel and worry about)."[37]

From this hadith, we understand:
- One can place their hand on the place of pain and recite.
- Regarding recitation on someone else, one is encouraged to place their hand on the place of pain or have a family member do it. If the person who is performing Ruqya a male, then he should not place his hand on a non-mahram.[38]
- Ruqya can be performed more than once and you can repeat duas and verses of the Qur'an for healing.

The Prophet (ﷺ) used to seek refuge in Allah from the evil eye of man and Jinn. In a hadith, Abu Saeed al-Khudri said, "The Messenger of Allah (ﷺ) used to seek refuge with Allah from the Jinn and from the evil eye until the Mu'awwidhatayn were revealed, and when they were revealed he started to recite them and not anything else."[39]

It was narrated that A'isha (may Allah be pleased with her) said: "When the Messenger of Allah (ﷺ) was ill, he would recite al-Mu'awwidhatayn (المعوذتان) over himself and spit drily. When

---

[37] Reported by Muslim

[38] A non-mahram is someone a Muslim can get married to.

[39] Reported An-Nasa'i

his pain grew intense in his final days, I recited over him and wiped him with his own hand, seeking its barakah (blessing)."[40]

From this hadith, we understand:
- It is Sunnah to spit drily before or after reciting and to wipe all over the body what your hands can reach.
- Even though the Prophet (ﷺ) was in pain, he did not stop Ruqya, he continued through the pain.
- A wife can perform Ruqya on her husband.
- If a person cannot perform Ruqya on himself or herself, another individual can perform Ruqya on the person for one reason or another.

It was narrated from A'isha (may Allah be pleased with her) that when the Messenger of Allah (ﷺ) came to a sick person or a sick person was brought to him, he would say,

أذهب الباس رب الناس اشف وأنت الشافي لا شفاء إلا شفاؤك شفاء لا يغادر سقماً

"Adhhib al-ba's Rabb an-naas, wa'shfi anta al-Shaafi, laa shifaa'a illa shifaa'uka shifaa'an laa yughaadir saqaman (Take away the pain, O Lord of mankind, and grant healing, for You are the Healer, and there is no healing but Your healing that leaves no trace of sickness)."[41]

From this hadith, we understand:
- It is advised to perform Ruqya for any type of illness.
- The Prophet used to perform Ruqya on others.
- When visiting a sick person, it is encouraged to do Ruqya on them.

---

[40] Reported by Bukhari and Muslim
[41] Reported by Bukhari and Muslim

Ruqya for the Evil-Eye of the Jinn *(Saf'ah, سَفْعَة)*

In a hadith narrated by Umm Salama: The Prophet (ﷺ) saw in her house a girl whose face had Saf'ah.[42] He said, "She is under the effect of an evil eye, Nadhara,[43] so treat her with Ruqya."

From this hadith, we understand:
- The Prophet ordered Ruqya to be performed on the young girl as she was suffering from the evil eye of the Jinn (Nadhara).

Al-Husayn ibn Mas'ood Al-Farraa' Al-Baghawee said: "An-nadhara is from the Jinn. He said that the young girl had An-Nadhara, evil eye, caused by the glance of a Jinni, which is more penetrating than the point of a spear."

From this, we understand that the evil eye of a Jinn is stronger than that of a human's. It is not only important to seek refuge from the evil eye of man but also that from the Jinn. Seeking refuge in Allah from the envier when he envies encompasses both of that from the man and the Jinn.

The Prophet (ﷺ) Ordered for Ruqya to Be Performed on Children

In a hadith narrated from Jabir ibn Abdullah: The Prophet (ﷺ) said to Asma bint Umays as follows, "Why do I see the sons of my brothers so weak? They seem they are in need of help." They were the sons of Jafar ibn Abu Talib. And Asma said, "They are not sick but they have been affected by evil eye."

---

[42] Saf'ah is a change of colour of the face or markings on the face of red or black, and Allah knows best.

[43] Nadhara is evil eye from the Jinn.

Upon this, the Messenger of Allah (ﷺ) said, "Then do Ruqya for them." [44]

From this hadith we understand:
- The first call of action from the Prophet was to perform Ruqya.
- Signs of weakness or being underweight can be from the evil eye.
- Children can become ill as a result of the evil eye.

The Prophet (ﷺ) Instructed for Ruqya to be Performed When It's Needed

Narrated from A'isha (may Allah be pleased with her) she said, "The Messenger of Allah (ﷺ) used to tell me to seek Ruqya for the evil eye."[45]

From this hadith, we understand:
- Ruqya is effective against the evil eye.
- There is nothing wrong with seeking Ruqya from others as long as it is needed and beneficial, and it meets the permissible conditions.

Ruqya for the Protection of Children

Ibn Abbas (may Allah be pleased with him) reported that the Prophet (ﷺ) would seek refuge for his grandsons Hasan and Hussain saying, "Verily, your forefather would seek refuge for Ishmael and Isaac":

أعيذكما بكلمات الله التامة من كل شيطان وهامة ، ومن كل عين لامة

---

[44] Reported by Muslim
[45] Reported by Bukhari and Muslim

"I seek refuge in the perfect Words of Allah from every devil and every poisonous reptile, and every bad eye."

From this hadith:

- Haammah means lethally poisonous animals and insects.
- Laammah is what causes harm because of jealousy (Hasad).
- Ruqya is a form of protection even though one may not be afflicted.
- Ruqya can be performed for children which is a Sunnah.
- The Prophet still sought refuge in Allah for his grandsons even though they were children and his relatives.

One Can Be Paid for Performing Ruqya

Narrated by Abu Sa'id Al-Khudri: Some of the companions of the Prophet (ﷺ) came across a tribe amongst the tribes of the Arabs, and that tribe did not entertain them. While they were in that state, the chief of that tribe was bitten by a snake (or stung by a scorpion). They said to the companions of the Prophet (ﷺ), "Have you got any medicine with you or anybody who can treat with Ruqya?" The Prophet's companions said, "You refuse to entertain us, so we will not treat your chief unless you pay us for it." So, they agreed to pay them a flock of sheep.[46] One of the Prophet's companions started reciting Surah Al-Fatiha and started gathering his saliva and spitting it at the wound. The patient got cured and his people presented the sheep to them. One of the companions said, "We will not take it unless we ask the Prophet whether it is lawful." When they asked the Prophet (ﷺ), he smiled and said, "How do you

---

[46] A flock of sheep is a group of sheep, usually of five or more.

know that Surah Al-Fatiha is a Ruqya? Take it (flock of sheep) and assign a share for me."[47]

From this hadith, we understand:

- Ruqya can be performed on non-Muslims.
- The Prophet smiled in approval and asked for a share of their payment to make them feel at ease and to let them know their action was permissible.
- The majority of scholars use this hadith as evidence for taking payment for Ruqya and for teaching the Qur'an. The Hanafis, however differed on taking payment for teaching Qur'an but accept it for Ruqya services. In addition, Bukhari said: Ibn Abbas said, "There is nothing more worthy of taking payment for than the Book of Allah."

Ruqya Can Be Performed on One Who is Possessed

On the authority of Kharajat bin As-Saalat and his uncle: We came from the Prophet (ﷺ), and we came across a tribe of Arabs who said, "It's come to our attention that you have come from this man, the Prophet (ﷺ), with good. Do you have any medicine or Ruqya (incantations)? Verily, we have a sick person chained up." We replied, "Yes, we have." They brought the person who was sick to us and I recited Surah Al-Fatiha for three days and nights and gathered my saliva and spat on him. It was as though he came back to normality. They gave me payment that I said no to until I asked the Prophet (ﷺ). He (ﷺ) replied "Eat from it. If anyone has taken payment for Ruqya that is lawful and true, verily you have."[48]

From this hadith, we understand:

---

[47] Reported by Bukhari
[48] Ahmad Musnad, Abu Dawud in The Book of Medicine, An-Nasa'i

- The person who was afflicted was restrained with chains. He was acting abnormal so the companion recited on him until he returned to his normal state.
- Ruqya can be performed on someone who is possessed.
- There is nothing wrong with repeating Ruqya or verses of the Qur'an and Du'as more than once.
- Again, taking payment for lawful Ruqya is permissible.

In conclusion:

- The Prophet (ﷺ) performed Ruqya on himself and on others.
- Ruqya was performed on the Prophet (ﷺ) and he (ﷺ) performed Ruqya on his family.
- He encouraged others to perform Ruqya and he ordered others to seek Ruqya as well.
- The hadiths highlight the virtues of the opening chapter of the Qur'an, Surah Al-Fatiha.
- Always refer back to people of knowledge when in doubt.
- One can take payment for performing the service of Ruqya.[49] The Prophet (ﷺ) asked for a share of the companion's payment to make him feel at ease. The Prophet (ﷺ) would not consume forbidden (haram) wealth or charity wealth.
- One can perform Ruqya without immense experience, however it is strongly advised to study under a professional Raqi and under scholars.
- Dry spitting, light wet spitting, wiping with one's hand, placing the hand over the place of pain, using water, repeating verses and supplications and blowing are all acceptable practices of Ruqya.

---

[49] Permanent Ifta' Committee, Islamic Research Journal, Issue 27, p. 57-58.

Chapter 10

Seeking Ruqya from Others

Narrated from Ibn 'Abbas (may Allah be pleased with him): The Messenger of Allah (ﷺ) said, "Seventy thousand of my Ummah will enter Paradise without being brought to account; they are the ones who did not ask for Ruqya or believe in omens or use cautery[50] and they put their trust in their Lord."[51]

This is a very important subject which has caused a lot of confusion, and has even stopped people from getting the correct advice, whereupon they have gone to psychiatrists, counselling, and all different types of therapy one can think of to no success. Some individuals, out of desperation, even turn to faith healers, charlatans, and magicians.

When they come across Ruqya, they become confused and do not want to seek it from others as they do not want to be left

---

[50] Cauterization is an old technique of a medical practice which burns a part of a body in attempts to remove, close off, stop bleeding or minimize infections.

[51] Reported by Bukhari and Muslim

out of the 70,000 who will enter Paradise without being held to account.

If we start looking at the reality of individuals, some individuals fall short in obligatory acts of worship and indulge heavily in sins. They are far away from the obedience to Allah and have been affected by an illness either from envy, evil eye, magic or Jinn possession. On top of that, they refuse to ask for Ruqya because they want to be among the 70,000 who enter into paradise without account. Individuals such as these who refuse seeking Ruqya, have misunderstood the above hadith because the reality of the 70,000 that the Prophet (ﷺ) spoke about are of those that are of the highest level of iman. The 70,000 individuals that are mentioned in the hadith are of high status and hold an honorable position in the sight of Allah. One can achieve this level of status, nobility, and iman. One must not use this hadith as an excuse when the correct help is needed.

As we read the hadith, we have to ask ourselves questions: Who are we putting our trust in, in Allah or in the Ruqya practitioner? Does our trust and faith in Allah increase? Do we find ourselves getting closer to Allah, or do we put faith in the healers, seeking their assistance because of their experience and knowledge of the matter?

Shaykh Ibn Baaz (may Allah have mercy on him) explains the above hadith as follows, "This hadith indicates that not asking is better, just as not using cautery is better, but when there is a need for it, there is nothing wrong with asking for ruqya or using cautery..."

This is a very important point highlighting when necessary, it is ok to ask for Ruqya as some people have left or neglected their Islamic duties because of their affliction. Their affliction leads them to the extent of divorce, the breaking up of families, falling into major sins, or leaving the fold of Islam altogether.

Shaykh Ibn Baaz then follows on to say, "...because the Messenger of Allah (ﷺ) told A'isha to ask for Ruqya for an illness that had befallen her, and he told the mother of the children of Ja'far ibn Abu Talib (may Allah be pleased with him), whose name was Asma bint 'Umays (may Allah be pleased with her), to perform Ruqya for them. This indicates that there is nothing wrong with that when there is a need."

These hadiths Shaykh Ibn Baaz mentioned is the same hadith we mentioned earlier in this book: Narrated from A'isha (may Allah be pleased with her) she said, "The Messenger of Allah (ﷺ) used to tell me to seek Ruqya for the evil eye."[52]

In another hadith the Shaykh mentioned: The Prophet (ﷺ) said to Asma bint Umays as follows, "Why do I see the sons of my brothers so weak? They seem they are in need of help." They were the sons of Jafar ibn Abu Talib. And Asma said, "They are not sick but they have been affected by evil eye. Shall I perform Ruqya on them?" She presented her Ruqya. Upon this, the Messenger of Allah (ﷺ) said, "Perform Ruqya for them."[53]

The scholars have different opinions on this matter. Each holds strongly to the opinion with evidence; however, I will break it down into five different views to make it simple for the reader to understand.

The Different Meanings of the "One Who Did Not Ask for Ruqya"

1. They do not ask anyone for Ruqya as they do not want their heart to turn towards the creation which is a contradiction to the total reliance on Allah. It does not

---

[52] Reported by Bukhari and Muslim
[53] Reported by Muslim narrated from Jabir ibn Abdullah

41

contradict medicine as it is not the subject matter, but the matter is Ruqya.

2. Another opinion is they do not ask anyone for Ruqya until the affliction happens which is ok to seek assistance in this situation.

3. The one who does not ask for Ruqya that was from the understanding of the pre-Islamic time as before Islam, people believed Ruqya had an effect within itself. However, if it meets the conditions then it is ok for the individual to ask for it.

4. The one who does not ask for Ruqya because it consists of Shirk (polytheism). This type of Ruqya was used during the pre-Islamic time. However, if it is with the words of Allah and that which is legal and accepted in Islam it is ok and does not fall into this category.

5. The one who does not ask for Ruqya unless one applies it to himself first and then seek it from others. This is ok because the individual is relying on Allah. If an individual does not apply Ruqya to themselves but rather they seek it from others without trying to do it to themselves first, it takes away the reliance and dependence on Allah. It glorifies the Raqi and the individual believes he has special healing powers.

All of this breakdown shows there is a difference of view on the matter.

The Different Types of Islamic Rulings in Seeking Ruqya

The Forbidden One
1. He is asking for Ruqya that is forbidden/asking other than Ruqya Shari'ah.
2. He has Ruqya performed on him believing that Ruqya has an effect in itself. This is wrong, and the

correct understanding is that the cure comes from Allah and not from the Ruqya itself.
3. He believes that the Raqi himself is the curer.

Seeking Ruqya that is Disliked
1. He gets Ruqya performed on him before any affliction.
2. He makes Ruqya as a normal practice, as a habit.
3. His heart is attached to the Raqi.

Seeking Ruqya Which is Allowed
1. Seeking Ruqya from someone who practices Ruqya Shari'ah
2. Seeking Ruqya in serious or desperate circumstances
3. Seeking Ruqya from a Raqi who has experience of these afflictions so one can learn and deal with these situations

Ruqya from the People of the Book (Disbelievers) and Mushrikeen (Polytheists)

Ruqya from among the non-Muslims can be from the Ahl Al-Kitab (People of the Book) whether they are Jews or Christians. In using their Ruqya, there is a difference of opinion amongst the scholars.

Imam Al-Shafi' was asked: "Can the people of the book perform Ruqya on the Muslims? He replied: Yes if their (means) of Ruqya is known within accordance of the Book of Allah or the remembrance of Allah.[54] I said (the questioner): And what is the evidence for this? Imam Al-Shafi' said: There is no evidence (which suggests otherwise), as for the narration of our friend and your friend (Referring to Imam Malik), Malik narrated that Yahya ibn Sa'eed narrated upon on the

---

[54] Refer back to chapter 8 Conditions of Permissible Ruqya

authority of Amrata the daughter of AbdulRahman that Abu Bakr (may Allah be pleased with him) entered upon A'isha (may Allah be pleased with her) while she was feeling pain and a Jewish woman was performing Ruqya upon her, So Abu Bakr (may Allah be pleased with him) replied: Make Ruqya for her from the Book of Allah. (The questioner) So I told Al-Shafi: We dislike the Ruqya of the people of the book, he (Al-Shafi') replied; why do you use this narration upon the authority of Abu Bakr and I do not know that you narrate another (Hadith) from one of the Companions of the Prophet (ﷺ) opposing this narration and Allah Glory be to He, has made permissible the food of the people of the Book and (marrying) their women and I see that the Ruqya if it was done (by them) through the book of Allah it would be similar to them or less.[55]

As for the Ruqya of the people of the Book, Imam Malik (may Allah have mercy on him) disliked it. Ibn Wahb however said: I do not dislike the Ruqya of the people of the Book and he based it on the hadith of Abu Bakr (may Allah be pleased with him), in that he said to Jewish woman: "Perform Ruqya with the Book of Allah (The Honourable, The Exalted)" and he (Ibn Wahb) did not take the dislikeness of Imam Malik on this issue.[56] As for the Ruqya of the Mushrikeen (Polytheists), it generally is not free of Shirk and supplications to other than Allah; therefore it is Haram unless it is completely free from Shirk. Sheikh Abdul-Aziz Ibn Baaz (may Allah have mercy on him) was asked the following question: Is it permissible for a Christian and Jew to perform Ruqya on a Muslim? He responded (may Allah have mercy on him): "If it was not from

---

[55] Al-Umm, by Al-Shafi'

[56] Al-Muntaqa; an Explanation of Al-Muwatta'

44

the people of war and it was within accordance to the Islamic Ruqya, it is permissible."[57]

The scholars of the Standing Committee issued a fatwa stating that that going to a Christian priest is not permissible, when they were asked:

The remedy for seizures among us in Egypt is to go to the church, especially the church of Mary Jarjis, or to go to practitioners of witchcraft and charlatans who are widespread in the villages. Sometimes that brings results. Is it permissible to do that? Please note that if the person who has a seizure is not treated quickly, he will die.

What is the remedy prescribed by Allah for this sickness, as there is a remedy for every disease except old age?

The scholars of the committee replied:

It is not permissible to go to the church to treat seizures, or to go to the practitioners of witchcraft or the charlatans. As for permissible remedies, he may be treated by means of ruqyas that are acceptable in Islam, such as reciting Qur'an, e.g., al-Fatiha, Qul Huwa Allahu Ahad (Surah Al-Ikhlas), Al-Mu'wadhatayn (the last two Surahs of the Qur'an in which refuge with Allah is sought) and Aayat Al-Kursi, as well as dhikrs and Du'a's that are soundly narrated from the Messenger (ﷺ). And Allah is the source of strength. End quote.

Fataawa al-Lajnah, 1/292-293

---

[57] Recorded Fatwa with the voice of the sheikh on 8th Sha'baan 1419Hj

Listening to Ruqya on an Electrical Device

From our experience and feedback, many individuals have found it helpful to listen to Ruqya on a tape, mobile phone or other device even though it is not from the origin of Ruqya as we understand it but because of the general meaning of the verse [Surah al-Isra' 17:82]. One must realise that reading, learning how to read Ruqya on oneself and following the reciter when he reads is better than simply listening to Ruqya on an electrical device. This does not fall under asking for Ruqya but rather all three conditions of Ruqya mentioned earlier in the book must be applied.

Shaykh Ibn Baaz (may Allah have mercy on him) issued a Fatwa stating that the recitation of Surah Al-Baqarah over the radio serves the purpose of driving the Shaytan away from the house.[58]

Listening to Ruqya in this manner is beneficial, in sha Allah. Many people have benefited from it, but this is not how it was performed in the past. It is best if the individual recites Qur'an himself or for someone else to recite it over him.

---

[58] Majmoo' Fataawa ash-Shaykh Ibn Baaz 24/413

Chapter 11

Ruqya from the Qur'an

Certain verses in the Qur'an have preference over other verses bearing in mind that the whole Qur'an is Shifa. Here are hadiths that highlight the virtues of certain chapters and verses.

Ruqya with Surah Al-Fatiha

A group of the companions of the Prophet (ﷺ) set out on a journey and travelled until they came near one of the Arab tribes. The companions asked the Arab tribe for hospitality, but they refused to do so. Then, the leader of that tribe was stung, and his people tried everything to no avail. Then, some of the tribe members said, "Why don't you go to those people who are staying (nearby)? Maybe some of them have something." So they went to the companions and said, "O people, our leader has been stung and we have tried everything, and nothing helped him. Do any of you have something? One of the companions said, "Yes, by Allah I will perform Ruqya for him, but by Allah we asked you for hospitality and you did not give us anything, so we will not perform Ruqya for you unless you give us something in return." So they agreed on a flock of sheep, then one of the companions started to blow on the chief of the tribe and recite Al-hamdu Lillaahi Rabb il-'Aalameen. Then, the chief recovered quickly from his complaint and started walking, and there was nothing wrong with him. Then the tribe handed the companions what they had agreed to, and some of them (the Sahabah) said, "Let us share it out." The one who had performed Ruqya said, "Do not do anything until we come to the Prophet (ﷺ) and tell him what happened, and we will wait and see what he tells us to do." So they came to the Messenger of Allah (ﷺ) and told him what had happened. He said, "How did you know that it is a Ruqya?" Then he (ﷺ) said, "You did the right thing. Share them out, and give me a share." And the Messenger of Allah (ﷺ) smiled.[59]

Ruqya with Surah Al-Baqarah

It was narrated that Abu Umaamah Al-Baahili said: I heard the Messenger of Allah (ﷺ) say, "Read Surah Al-Baqarah, for reciting it regularly is a blessing and forsaking it is a cause of regret, and the magicians cannot withstand it."

It was narrated from Abu Hurayrah that the Messenger of Allah (ﷺ) said: "Do not make your houses into graves, for the Shaytaan flees from a house in which Surah Al-Baqarah is recited."

Ruqya with Aayat Al-Kursi

It was reported that Abu Hurayrah (may Allah be pleased with him) said: The Messenger of Allah (ﷺ) put me in charge of guarding the Zakah of Ramadan. Someone came and started to scatter the food. I took hold of him and said, "I will take you

---

[59] Reported by Bukhari and Muslim

to the Messenger of Allah (ﷺ).".... He said, "When you go to bed, recite Aayat Al-Kursi and you will be protected by Allah, and no Shaytan (devil) will come near you until morning." The Prophet (ﷺ) said, "He told you the truth even though he is a liar. That was a Shaytan."[60]

Ruqya with the last two Ayahs of Surah Al-Baqarah

It was reported that Abu Mas'ood Al-Badri (may Allah be pleased with him) said: The Messenger of Allah (ﷺ) said, "The last two ayahs of Surah Al-Baqarah – whoever recites them at night, they will be sufficient for him."[61]

Ruqya with Al-Mu'awwidhat

It was narrated that A'isha (may Allah be pleased with her) said: When the Messenger of Allah (ﷺ) was ill, he would recite al-Mu'awwidhat over himself and spit drily. When his pain grew intense, I recited over him and wiped him with his own hand, seeking its barakah (blessing).[62]

---

[60] Reported by Bukhari
[61] Reported by Bukhari
[62] Reported by Bukhari and Muslim

Chapter 12

Selected Ruqya from the Sunnah

In Sahih Muslim, Abu Hurayrah (may Allah be pleased with him) said: A man came to the Prophet (ﷺ) and said, "O Messenger of Allah, I was stung by a scorpion last night." He (ﷺ) said, "If you had said, when evening came,

أعوذ بكلمات الله التامات من شر ما خلق

A'oodhu bi kalimaat Allaah al-taammah min sharri ma khalaq

I seek refuge in the perfect words of Allah from the evil of that which He has created, it would not have harmed you."[63]

---

[63] Reported by Muslim

Other similar Du'as mentioned in other hadiths include:

أعوذ بكلمات الله التامة من غضبه وعقابه ، ومن شر عباده ومن
همزات الشياطين وأن يحضرون

*A'oodhu bi kalimat-illah il-tammati min ghadabihi wa 'iqabihi, wa min
sharri 'ibadihi wa min hamazat al-shayateeni wa an yahduroon*

I seek refuge in the perfect words of Allah from His wrath
and punishment, from the evil of His slaves and from the evil
promptings of the devils and from their presence.[64]

It was reported that Abu Hurayrah (may Allah be pleased with
him) said: Abu Bakr said, "O Messenger of Allah, teach me
something that I can say in the morning and in the evening."
He (ﷺ) said, "Say,

اللهم عالم الغيب والشهادة فاطر السموات والأرض ربَّ كلِّ شيءٍ
ومليكه أشهد أن لا إله إلا أنت أعوذ بك من شرِّ نفسي ومِن شرِّ
الشيطان وشِركه

*Allaahumma 'Aalim al-ghaybi wa'l-shahaadah, Faatir al-samawaati
wa'l-ard, Rabba kulli shay'in wa maleekahu, ashhadu an laa ilaaha
illa anta. A'oodhi bika min sharri nafsi wa min sharr il-shaytaan wa
shirkih*

O Allah, Knower of the seen and the unseen, Creator of the
heavens and the earth, Lord and Sovereign of all things, I
bear witness that there is no god except You. I seek refuge in
You from the evil of my own self and from the evil and shirk

---

[64] Abu Dawud, Albanee, Sahih At-Tirmidhi

51

of the Shaytaan. Say this in the morning and in the evening, and when you go to bed."[65]

It was narrated from Aban ibn Uthman that his father said:

The Messenger of Allah (ﷺ) said, "Whoever says

بِسْمِ اللَّهِ الَّذِي لَا يَضُرُّ مَعَ اسْمِهِ شَيْءٌ فِي الْأَرْضِ وَلَا فِي السَّمَاءِ وَهُوَ السَّمِيعُ الْعَلِيمُ

Bismillah illadhi la yadurru ma'a ismihi shay'un fi'l-ard wa la fi'l-sama' wa huwa al-samee' ul-'aleem

In the name of Allah with Whose name nothing can harm on earth or in heaven, and He is the All-Hearing, All-Knowing, nothing will harm him".[66]

And one may recite the words of Allah:

حسبي الله لا إله إلا هو عليه توكلت وهو رب العرش العظيم

Hasbi Allahu la ilaha illa huwa, 'alayhi tawakkaltu wa huwa Rabb ul-'arsh il-'azeem

Allah is sufficient for me. None has the right to be worshipped but He. In Him I put my trust and He is the Lord of the Mighty Throne.[67]

---

[65] Reported by Tirmidhi, Abu Dawood
[66] Reported by Abu Dawood
[67] Interpretation of Surah At-Tawbah 9:129

It was narrated from A'isha (may Allah be pleased with her) that when any of us fell sick, the Messenger of Allah (ﷺ) would wipe him with his right hand then say:

أَذهِبِ البَاسَ ، رَبَّ النَّاسِ ، وَاشفِ أَنتَ الشَّافِي ، لَا شِفَاءَ إلا شِفَاؤُكَ ، شِفَاءً لَا يُغَادِرُ سَقَمًا

Adhhib il-ba's, Rabbi l-naas washfi anta al-Shaafi laa shifaa'a illa shifaa'uka shifaa'an laa yughaadir saqaman.

Remove the harm, O Lord of mankind and heal him, for You are the Healer and there is no healing except Your healing, with a healing which does not leave any disease behind.[68]

It was narrated from 'Uthman ibn Abi'l-'Aas al-Thaqafi that he complained to the Messenger of Allah (ﷺ) about some pain that he had felt in his body since he became Muslim. The Messenger of Allah (ﷺ) said to him, "Put your hand on the part of your body that hurts and say, 'Bismillah (in the name of Allah)' three times, then say seven times:

بِاسمِ اللهِ ، أَعُوذُ بِاللهِ وَقُدرَتِهِ مِن شَرِّ مَا أَجِدُ وَأُحَاذِرُ

A'oodhu Billaahi wa qudratihi min sharri ma ajid wa uhaadhir

'I seek refuge in Allah and His Power from the evil of what I find and I fear.'"[69]

---

[68] Reported by Bukhari and Muslim
[69] Reported by Muslim

It was narrated from Abu Sa'eed al-Khudri (may Allah be pleased with him) that Jibreel (peace be upon him) came to the Prophet (ﷺ) and said, "O Muhammad, are you sick?" He (ﷺ) said, "Yes." Jibreel then said,

بِاسْمِ اللهِ أَرْقِيكَ ، مِن كُلِّ شَيْءٍ يُؤْذِيكَ ، مِن شَرِّ كُلِّ نَفْسٍ أَو عَيْنٍ
حَاسِدٍ ، اللَّهُ يَشْفِيكَ ، بِاسْمِ اللَّهِ أَرْقِيكَ

Bismillahi arqeeka min kulli shayin yudheeka, min sharri kulli nafsin aw 'aynin hasid Allaahu yashfeek, bismillahi arqeek

"In the name of Allah I perform ruqyah for you, from everything that is harming you, from the evil of every soul or envious eye may Allah heal you, in the name of Allah, I perform ruqyah for you."[70]

It was narrated that Abu'l-Darda' (may Allah be pleased with him) said: I heard the Messenger of Allah (ﷺ) say, "Whoever among you suffers some sickness, or his brother suffers some sickness, let him say

رَبَّنَا اللَّهُ الذِي فِي السَّمَاءِ ، تَقَدَّسَ اسْمُكَ ، أَمْرُكَ فِي السَّمَاءِ وَالأَرْضِ ،
كَمَا رَحْمَتُكَ فِي السَّمَاءِ فَاجْعَلْ رَحْمَتَكَ فِي الأَرْضِ ، اغْفِر لَنَا حَوْبَنَا
وَخَطَايَانَا ، أَنتَ رَبُّ الطَّيِّبِينَ ، أَنزِلْ رَحْمَةً مِن رَحْمَتِكَ ، وَشِفَاءً مِن
شِفَائِكَ عَلَى هَذَا الوَجَعِ ، فَيَبَرَأَ

Rabuna Lahu al ladi fi sama taqadasa ismukaamruka fi sama i wal ardi kama rahmatuka fi sama i faj'al rahmataka fil ardi ighfir lana hawbana wa khatayana anta Rabu attayyibin anzil rahmatan min rahmatik wa shifa an min shifa ika 'ala hadal waj 'i fa yabra.

[70] Reported by Muslim

Our Lord Allah Who is in heaven, hallowed be Your name, You will is done in heaven and on earth; as Your mercy is in heaven, bestow it upon the earth. Forgive us our sins. You are the Lord of the good. Send down some Your mercy and healing upon this pain,' and he will be healed."[71]

It was narrated from Ibn 'Abbas (may Allah be pleased with him) that the Prophet (ﷺ) said, "The one who visits a sick person who is not dying, and says seven times in his presence,

$$أَسأَلُ اللَّهَ العَظِيمَ رَبَّ العَرشِ العَظِيمِ أَن يَشفِيَكَ$$

As aluLuha al 'adima Raba al'arshi al 'adimi ayshfika

'I ask Allah the Almighty, the Lord of the Mighty Throne, to heal you,' Allah will heal him from that sickness."[72]

Three Important Points to Remember

1. *Intention:* One must check their intention or renew their intention for Ruqya. The intention should be to ask Allah to remove all evil and to heal oneself completely.
2. *Conviction:* One should have full faith that Allah will answer their requests.
3. *Patience and Consistency:* One should be patient and consistent with Ruqya treatment and not be hasty in resolving the ailment.

---

[71] Reported by Abu Dawood; classed as saheeh by al-Haakim in al-Mustadrak and as hasan by Ibn Taymiyah in Majmoo' al-Fataawa,

[72] Narrated by Abu Dawood; classed as saheeh by al-Nawawi in al-Adhkaar (p. 180) and by al-Albaani in Saheeh Abi Dawood

Etiquettes of Performing Ruqya on Oneself

One can make wudu, offer two rakahs, pray tahajjud, make astaghfaar, and face the Qiblah.

While facing the Qiblah, one can start to perform Ruqya on oneself by beginning with praising Allah and sending salutations to the Prophet (ﷺ). One can recite the verses and Du'as more than once and blow on his hands and wipe over his body.

For a more in-depth action plan, please refer to the treatment programs towards the end of the book.

Chapter 13

Preparing the Home for Ruqya

Many people complain of paranormal activities taking place in the home: doors opening and closing on their own, hearing voices or knocks or thuds, having items go missing or reappearing in different places, smelling a strange odor whether pleasant or unpleasant, lights flickering or turning on and off on their own. Some even complain that they see smoke, shadow figures, fast-moving lights or feel a presence.

Before starting your Ruqya treatment program, it is very important to prepare your home for Ruqya.

How to Prepare the Home:
1. Remove all images and statues of animals or human beings.
2. Make sure there are no dogs in the house.
3. Do not play music in the house or anything that is impermissible.
4. Recite Surah Al-Baqarah in the house every three days or play the audio daily.
5. Say Bismillah before entering and exiting the house.
6. Remove any taweez (paper amulets).

7. Remove any evil eye amulets hanging in the house such as the blue eye, horseshoe, rabbit's foot, good luck charms, etc.
8. Spray the house with Ruqya water.
9. Play the Adhan in the house or recite it out loud regularly.
10. You can also say "Leave in the name of Allah. You have no right to be here" if you feel a presence.

How to Prepare Ruqya Water:

1. Bring the container of water close to your mouth.
2. Recite Surah Al-Fatiha, Surah Al-Ikhlas, Surah Al-Falaq, Surah An-Nas, Ayatul Kursi, the last two ayahs of Surah Al-Baqarah and any other verses you would like to include. You can find these verses at the back of this book. Blow on the water.
3. Lightly spray the house, the beds, sofas, the doors with Ruqya water. You can add rose water to it as well for a nice fragrance.

Chapter 14

Breaking Free from Affliction

The earlier you start your self-Ruqya treatment plan, the sooner you will see positive results.

Train Your Brain: You can steer yourself to any direction you choose, so stay focused. You may find the first initial phase difficult but adherence to the self-Ruqya treatment plan is essential towards positive outcomes, and for you to take an active role in managing your affliction.

Think Ahead: Plan out a time slot for your self-Ruqya.

Don't Skip: Make it a priority to stay consistent and do Ruqya daily. Stick to the regimen and persevere. Maintaining self-Ruqya is crucial for success in-sha-Allah.

Pulling It All Together: Keeping a journal or diary can help assess your illness, help you track your progress and chart what emotions you are feeling during the day. All of this information gives you a clearer picture of how your self-Ruqya is working and will help you manage your affliction.

Do Not Give Up: Shaytan may give you waswas making you think you are going to find doing Ruqya too hard and that it will get in the way of your work and other daily tasks. Ignore these negative thoughts and carry on with your Ruqya.

Seek the Help of Allah and Do Not Feel Helpless: Do not feel weak against your enemy as Allah 'Azza Wa Jal Says: "... weak indeed is the plot of shaytan ..." [Interpretation of Surah an-Nisa 4:76].

"I Can Do It!" Attitude: Look at your situation with a positive light. Keep your thoughts positive and challenge negativity by seeking refuge with Allah.

Chapter 15

Questions & Answers Concerning Ruqya

Drinking Water Recited On, Washing the Body with It & Performing Ruqya Unto Those in Menstruation

Question: What is the validity of drinking or washing the body with the water on which Qur'anic verses have been recited? Is it allowed to perform Ruqyas unto those in menstruation, Nifas (parturition) or Janabah (the state after intercourse when one has not washed yet)?

Answer: In the case of Janabah, patients have to do Ghusl (have a bath/shower) so as to be ready for receiving Ruqya treatment, even if it is only drinking or washing with water on which recitation has been done. This is believed to render treatment more effective.

In the cases of Haidh[73] and Nifas, females can use water recited unto, for delaying the ruqya treatment till Haidh or Nifas is over can be harmful.

---

[73] Haidh in Arabic means menstruation.

Treatment Lies in Remembrance of Allah, Patience, etc.

Question: Some man fell ill, but ordinary medical treatment did not work with him. When he got treatment with a Ruqya, his condition improved, but afterwards he relapsed. He is now asking, —What is the treatment in my case?

Answer: Generally speaking, treatment requires two things. The first one is the trust in and the love of what is good. The second is that one ought to patiently endure his suffering and to consider it as a test for measuring one's patience by Allah. If one patiently endures suffering, one receives support and reward from Allah, for He says, "Verily the steadfast will be paid their wages without stint."

In this patient's particular case, we recommend the following: Firstly, he should do as many good deeds as possible, such as Salat, supplications, reading the Qur'an and other forms of worship.

Secondly, he should attend assemblies for Allah's remembrance and religious seminars, such activities bring about comfort on the one hand, and keep alien thoughts away from him on the other. Thirdly, he should keep doing useful things, which can be a source of comfort to him. For instance, he could listen to audio material or read material of an Islamic nature, such as sermons, teachings, verdicts, stories and parables etc. If he does all the above, the general and the particular, and gets treatment with Ruqyas according to the Qur'an and the Sunnah, we trust that Allah will ease his suffering.

Al-Jibreen, Al-Kinz Aththmeen (The Precious Treasure), p. 210-211.

Lustful Jinn

Shaykh 'Abdullah al-Jibreen (may Allah have mercy on him) said: Some of the Jinn may appear to a man in the form of a woman, then the human has intercourse with her, or a Jinni may appear in the form of a man and have intercourse with a human woman, as a man has intercourse with a woman.

The remedy for that is: to protect oneself from them, both male and female, by means of the Du'as and Awraad[74] narrated in the religious texts, and reciting verses that speak of seeking protection and guarding against them, by Allah's leave.

End quote from *Fataawa 'Ulama' al-Balad al-Haraam*, p. 1546

Can a Person Who Says Adhkaar Be Possessed by Jinn?

Shaykh Saalih al-Fawzaan (may Allah preserve him) was asked: We find that some people are affected by possession or the evil eye even though they protect themselves with adhkaar in the morning and evening. What is the guideline concerning that?

He replied: If Allah wills that something should befall him, the person will fail to recite dhikr on that day; either he will forget it or he will be distracted from it.[75]

Those Who Do Not Believe the Qur'an is a Healing

Question: What about those who do not believe in the healing power of the Qur'an, who consider treatment by it as a myth

---

[74] Awraad means a portion of the Qur'an that you read on a regular basis or the morning and evening supplications.

[75] https://www.alfawzan.af.org.sa/ar/node/14626

and who believe that proper treatment has to be done only by material means as in medical practice?

Answer: To believe that the Qur'an is not a healing contradicts the Qur'an and the Hadith. In the Qur'an, Allah says, "and we reveal of the Qur'an that which is a healing and a mercy to believers."[76] He says also, "Say: It [the Qur'an] is for those who believe [in it] a guidance and a healing."[77] The Hadith reports the case of the Sahabi (the Prophet's Companion) who treated a patient stung by a scorpion. The patient was cured and was able to walk without any suffering after the Ruqya treatment.[78] Many other successful cases have been reported. Experience tells us that some illnesses which are too difficult for skilful doctors to treat by known medical means (medications and operations) have been - by Allah's permission - effectively treated with Ruqyas.

Obviously, some medical doctors, by the nature of their training, are likely to deny that people can be possessed by the devil or be affected by magic or envy. Since such causes cannot be materially identified by ordinary medical tools, such as the stethoscope, the microscope and x-rays, patients are judged as physically sound in spite of their epileptic fits, fainting and inner suffering, which disturb them and cause sleeplessness and restlessness.

However, once those very patients are treated by means of legal Ruqyas, their suffering is – by Allah's permission - removed. How effective Ruqyas are is related to the religious states of Raqis and patients. Regarding the Raqi, much depends on his mastery of relevant prayers and Qur'anic verses and on his faith, honesty, purity of intention and avoidance of suspicious deeds. Patients, on the other hand,

---

[76] Surah Al-Isra 17:82
[77] Surah Al-Fussilat 41:44
[78] Reported by Bukhari and Muslim

must be committed Muslims, who believe in the oneness of Allah and shun sins. Such qualities of Raqis and patients should – by Allah's permission – produce good results.[79]

Jibreel Descends When Treating Some Jinn-Possessed Cases Is Unfounded

Question: Some people in our area treat Jinn-possessed cases by Qur'anic recitations. They have claimed that when they were treating one such case, Jibreel came down from the sky and helped them to drive the Jinni out of the patient. This claim has created dissension and confusion among people.
Will you please give us a clear and simple explanation to this issue? Has Jibreel come down to help anybody or for any other purpose since the death of Allah's Messenger?

Answer: It is legitimate to treat Jinn-possessed patients with Qur'anic recitations (be they verses from one Sura, a whole Sura or Suras), for using the Qur'an for Ruqyas is a legally established Islamic practice. Regarding Jibreel's descending, this is a totally unfounded claim. [80]

The Legality of Ruqya and Amulets

Question: What is the legality of Ruqyas and Amulets?

Answer: Ruqyas are legitimate so long as they use the Qur'an, Allah's Attributes, the Prophet's established prayers and other similar prayers in the belief that they are only a means and that only Allah, the Exalted, is the source of all harm, all benefit and all healing. The Prophet (ﷺ) himself performed Ruqyas unto others and received them as well. He (ﷺ) says, "Ruqyas

---

[79] A Fatawa by Al-Jibreen, signed by him
[80] Ifta' Permanent Committee, Islamic Research Journal, Issue 27, pp. 52-53.

are valid so long as they are void of Shirk." Therefore, if they violate this requirement, they are forbidden.

As for amulets, according to relevant Hadiths, they are not allowed even if they are from the Qur'an.[81]

Employment of the Jinn & Confining Patients

Question: This is a question sent by Humud Jabir Al-Mubarak from Riyadh: Sometimes, if a person falls ill with Sara' (epilepsy/madness), his family take him to those who employ the Jinn and who perform strange activities. For example, they put the patient in solitary confinement for a period of time, after which they say that he is possessed, under the effect of magic or something in that line of diagnosis. After treatment and after the patient is healed, wages are paid to those who administered the treatment.

What is the legality of all this?

What is the legality of treatment with incantations in which are written Qur'anic verses and which are soaked into water to be drunk?

Answer: The treatment of Sara' and magic with Qur'anic verses and allowed remedies is valid so long as it is administered by a person known for good faith and committed to Shari'ah teachings.

However, those who claim to know the unseen or employ the Jinn as well as sorcerers and those whose status and treatment methods are shrouded with mysteries must not be consulted or approached for treatment. About such people the Prophet (ﷺ)

---

[81] Fatawa of the Ifta' Permanent Committee, Vol. 1, p. 207.

says, "If one consults a soothsayer, his prayers will not be accepted for forty days."[82] He also says, "If one consults soothsayers or charlatans and believes what they tell him, he is a disbeliever in what has been revealed to Muhammad."[83]

Besides, there are other Hadiths on that issue. All of them prohibit consulting or believing soothsayers and charlatans, who claim to know the unseen or employ the Jinn, and whose activities are indicative of their alien thoughts. It is such people that are condemned in the Hadith which Jabir narrated: The Prophet (ﷺ) was asked about the legality of Annashrah, and he said, "It is from Satan."[84] By Annashrah is meant the magical practices prevalent in the Jahili (pre-Islamic) era, such as treatment of magic with counter-magic and treatment sought from soothsayers, charlatans and sorcerers. Thus, treatment of diseases, including Sara', is valid only by Shar'i (lawful) means, of which are Qur'anic recitations, Nafth[85] and the Prophet's established prayers. In this respect, the Prophet (ﷺ) says, "Ruqyas are valid so long as they are void of Shirk."[86] He (ﷺ) also says, "O slaves of Allah, seek medications (for your illnesses), but do not use forbidden materials."[87]

As for writing Qur'anic verses or established prayers, using, for example, saffron, in a clean bowl or on clean paper, to be washed by water, which is to be drunk by the patient, it is allowed so long as it is done by those known for their righteousness and good behaviour. Such treatment was done

---

[82] Reference for hadith has given in previous chapters
[83] Reference for hadith has given in previous chapters
[84] Reference for hadith has given in previous chapters
[85] Nafth is blowing with dry spit
[86] Reference for hadith has given in previous chapters
[87] Reference for hadith has given in previous chapters

by a lot of Salaf,[88] as explained by Ibn-Al-Qayyim in Zad Al-Ma'ad and in other books.[89]

Treatment of Psychological Diseases with Ruqya

Question: Do believers become psychologically ill? What is a legitimate treatment for such diseases? Mind you, modern medicine treats them with modern medications only.

Answer: No doubt man gets psychologically sick, as he worries about the future and grieves about the past. Psychological diseases can affect the body more badly than physical diseases. Treating such diseases by means of Shar'i Ruqyas is better than treatment with physical medications as we know them.

Some of the Ruqyas for treating psychological diseases are:

As narrated by Ibn-Mas'ud, the Prophet (ﷺ) said, "If any believer afflicted with distress or grief makes this supplication, Allah will remove it: O Allah, I am Your servant, son of Your man-servant, son of Your woman-servant. My forehead is in Your hand. Your command concerning me prevails, and Your decision concerning me is just. O Allah, by every one of the names by which You have described Yourself, or which You have revealed in Your book, or which You have taught anyone of Your creatures, or which You have chosen to keep in the knowledge of the unseen with You, I pray You to make the Qur'an the delight of my heart, the light of my breast, and the remover of my grief, sorrow, and distress."

One can also say, "There is no god but You, You are far exalted and above all weaknesses, and I was indeed the wrongdoer."

---

[88] Salaf in Arabic means pious predecessors
[89] Ifta' Permanent Committee, Fatwas on Treatment Using the Qur'an and the Sunnah, Ruqyas and Related Issues, by Ibn-Baz and Ibn-Uthaimeen, pp.31-33.

For further prayers, one can read supplication books, such as Ibn-Al-Qayyim's Al-Wabil Assayyib and Zad-Al-Ma'ad, Ibn-Taymiyya's Al-Kalim Attayyib and Annawawi's Al-Adhkar.

However, on the one hand, now that people's faith is weak, they are reluctant to seek Shar'i treatment (faith healing). Instead, they have become more dependent on physical medications. On the other hand, when faith was strong, they sought Shar'i treatment, which was very effective, actually more effective than the ordinary physical one. This is clearly reflected in the well-known story of some of the Prophet's companions.

According to the story, the companions camped near one of the Arab tribes. They requested the tribe to entertain them as their guests, but the tribesmen refused. When the tribe's chief was bitten by snake, some tribesmen said, "Will you go to those who have dismounted nearby and see if there is a Raqi among them?" When approached, the companions replied, "We will not treat your patient till you fix for us some sheep as wages." A deal was struck. One companion went with the tribesmen and performed a Ruqya by reciting Al-Fatiha only. The patient was healed and started walking as if he had not been sick. Thus, the Fatiha was effective because it was recited by a Muslim whose heart was full of faith. When told the story, the Prophet (ﷺ) said, "How did you know that it (Al-Fatiha) is a Ruqya?"[90]

Nowadays, faith is so weak that on one extreme, people have become dependent on material treatment. On the other extreme, there are those sorcerers, who have been deceiving and misleading people into believing that they are innocent Raqis, but this is not true; they are taking people's money unlawfully. Thus, there are those people who have completely

---

[90] Reference for hadith has been given in previous chapters.

69

lost faith in Ruqyas, those involved in magic, and those in between.[91]

Diagnosis of Illness

Question: Can the Raqi tell if an illness is devil possession or something else?

Answer: Obviously, the experienced Raqi has examined and treated such varied cases as well as similar ones that he has become skilful at diagnosing psychological illness through his knowledge of their typical symptoms. However, not all Raqis do have such knowledge. Some Raqis may claim to have it, but in fact they do not, for they depend, when diagnosing, on mere guessing, not on proven knowledge. Wallahu-A'Iam (The truth of the matter is only with Allah).

A Fatawa by Al-Jibreen, signed by him

---

[91] Ifta' Permanent Committee, Fatwas on Treatment Using the Qur'an and the Sunnah, Ruqyas and Related Issues, by Ibn-Baaz and Ibn-Uthaimeen, pp. 22-24.

Chapter 16

Evil Eye & Envy

It is from the consensus of Ahl al-Sunnah wal-Jama'ah[92] and by real-life encounters witnessed around the world that the evil eye is real and has a harmful effect on all aspects life.

Allah speaks about the evil eye and envy in numerous places in the Qur'an:

وَمِن شَرِّ حَاسِدٍ إِذَا حَسَدَ

"And from the evil of an envier when he envies" [Interpretation of Surah Al-Falaq 113:5].

وَإِن يَكَادُ ٱلَّذِينَ كَفَرُوا لَيُزْلِقُونَكَ بِأَبْصَٰرِهِمْ لَمَّا سَمِعُوا ٱلذِّكْرَ وَيَقُولُونَ إِنَّهُۥ لَمَجْنُونٌ

"And indeed, those who disbelieve would almost make you slip with their eyes [i.e., looks] when they hear the message, and they say, 'Indeed, he is mad'" [Interpretation of Al-Qalam 68:52].

In a hadith narrated from A'isha (May Allah be pleased with her), she said, "The Messenger of Allah (ﷺ) used to tell me to seek ruqyah for the evil eye."[93]

In another hadith narrated from Abdullah ibn Abbas (May Allah be pleased with him) he said that the Prophet (ﷺ) said, "The evil eye is real and if anything were to overtake the divine decree, it would have been the evil eye. When you are asked to take a bath (as a cure) from the influence of the evil eye, you should take a bath."[94]

The one who is afflicted with the evil eye should wash their body with the water from the one who gave them the evil eye.

Signs and Symptoms

For the one who is afflicted with the evil eye, there are certain signs during the day, while they are asleep, before Ruqya treatment and during Ruqya treatment. All of these and after the treatment, need to be taken into account when diagnosing someone correctly. If someone has one or few of the symptoms mentioned below, it does not mean they have the evil eye. One must always consult a professional Raqi or medical practitioner who can correctly diagnose.

Generally speaking this is a small guide:

- Hot and cold flushes for no medical reason

---

[93] Reported by Bukhari and Muslim
[94] Reported by Muslim, Ahmad, Tirmidhi

- Constant yawning without wanting sleep. You will find it very strange when a person starts yawning when the Qur'an is being recited on him especially when the issue of evil eye is mentioned or what they have been given the evil eye on such as money, wealth, children, beauty, education etc. This happens with many cases and with many different practitioners.
- Constant burping without eating at the time when the Qur'an is being recited especially when the issue of evil eye is mentioned or what they have been given the evil eye on.
- Severe itching that starts when a person carries out an act for which the evil eye has been given on or when the issue on what they have evil eye on is mentioned. For example, if the evil eye has been given because of a person's wealth, they will start itching when they come into contact with money or hear Qur'anic verses regarding wealth.
- Tight chested, especially towards or during the evening
- Tiredness, Laziness, Apathy when doing the activity that the evil eye has been given on
- Insomnia, they feel really tired but when they try to go to sleep, they can't
- Constant forgetfulness and sleepiness
- Headaches for no medical reason
- Permanent headaches, migraines without medical cause
- Allergies, rhinitis and sinusitis that come out from nowhere
- Sneezing a lot for no reason when Qur'an is recited
- Cold, flu even during the summer or feel run down after being somewhere or at a gathering

- Putting on weight without necessarily eating more or losing weight with no medical reason
- Some cases of cancer or rare illnesses
- Pains at the mouth of the stomach which doctors cannot explain
- All physical ailments which doctors cannot explain, the illness/pain moves from one part of the body to another part of the body
- Hair loss for no reason
- Appearance of spots and boils on the person's body
- Darkening under the eyes
- Becoming pale
- Spots under the skin
- Waswasah, intrusive thoughts
- Some cases of psychological conditions such as delusion, fear, paranoia
- The desire to get out of the house or hatred in staying in the house
- The feeling of death and despair, hopelessness
- Seeing ants or any other infestation of insects appearing in the house
- Children crying constantly for no reason

Dreams
- Seeing dead people in your sleep
- Seeing creatures with red or blue eyes
- Hearing someone in your dream telling you that you have the evil eye
- Seeing people who have given you the evil eye looking at you in a strange and scary way
- Seeing loads of faces or people staring at you
- Seeing certain animals in your dreams
- Seeing lizards
- Seeing mice and rats

- Seeing cats, kittens or big cats such as lions, leopards, tigers etc.
- Seeing crocodiles or alligators
- Seeing insects such as spiders, ants, centipedes etc.

The signs and symptoms mentioned are just a few. It depends on the individual. Some people do not see many dreams until they start Ruqya and things become clearer through their dreams. A Raqi will put everything together to determine a diagnosis: a person's dreams and their symptoms before, during and after Ruqya.

Treatment Plan for Evil Eye & Envy

1. The Sunnah method is to wash oneself from the water of the wudu of the person who gave you Ayn (if the identity of the person is known). If you do not know who gave the Ayn or their water is not available, then wash with Ruqya water that is recited on as many times a day as possible (3-4 times is good).

2. Recite Surah Al-Baqarah once daily (twice or three times a day if possible). For those that struggle with the recitation itself or with difficulty completing the recitation during one session, it is advised to listen to an audio recitation and put your finger on the words of the Mushaf as you follow the recitation.

3. Recite Aayat Al-Kursi, Surah Al-Falaq and Surah An-Nas throughout the day (even while doing chores, shopping, etc.)

4. Recite the verses of Ayn. If you were reading and/or memorizing Qur'an before you were afflicted, then continue to do as before you were afflicted and memorize the same amount with the intention of Ruqya.

5. Listen to the Ruqya audio of Ayn on our website https://alruqya.com/sound/.You can also download our app: Ruqya Healing Guide.

6. If the Ayn is related to education then in addition to the above, listen to the knowledge (Ilm) audio which can be found on our site. Some signs of having the evil eye on one's knowledge, intelligence, education include inability to read or study, difficulty focusing or sleepiness during studies and readings, poor academic performance, etc.

7. Recite daily words of remembrance in the morning and evening (adhkaar). This is very important and cannot be stressed enough.

Chapter 17

Black Magic (Sihr)

It is from the consensus of Ahl al-Sunnah wal-Jama'ah and by real-life encounters witnessed around the world that magic is real and has a harmful effect on all aspects life.

Allah Says:

وَٱتَّبَعُواْ مَا تَتْلُواْ ٱلشَّيَٰطِينُ عَلَىٰ مُلْكِ سُلَيْمَٰنَ

"And they followed [instead] what the devils had recited during the reign of Solomon" [Interpretation of Surah Al-Baqarah 2:102].

قَالَ أَلْقُواْ فَلَمَّآ أَلْقَوْاْ سَحَرُواْ أَعْيُنَ ٱلنَّاسِ وَٱسْتَرْهَبُوهُمْ وَجَآءُو بِسِحْرٍ عَظِيمٍ

"He said, 'Throw,' and when they threw, they bewitched the eyes of the people and struck terror into them, and they presented a great [feat of] magic" [Interpretation of Surah Al-A'raf 7:118].

The Prophet (ﷺ) said, "Avoid the seven destructive things." It was asked (by those present), "What are they, O Messenger of Allah?" He replied, "Associating anyone or anything with Allah in worship; practising sorcery magic,..."[95]

There are many evidences that magic is real, and it is something that one should be cautious of and stay away from. Seek Allah's protection from it as Allah ordered the Prophet to seek refuge in Him from it: *"And from the evil of those witches casting spells by blowing onto knots"* [Interpretation of Surah Al-Falaq 113:4]. It is important to keep in mind that magic does not happen except by the will of Allah: *"But they do not harm anyone through it except by permission of Allah"* [Interpretation of Surah Al-Baqarah 2:102].

Signs and Symptoms

The signs and symptoms of one who is afflicted with magic vary from one to another. The magic tries to influence someone to do certain things or abstain from certain things. It can even cause illness or death. Depending on the person's religious commitment and strength, the symptoms will vary. The symptoms show before Ruqya, during, and after as well as when one is awake or asleep. The majority of time, a person who is afflicted by magic will be possessed by a Jinni or a group of Jinn to influence him or her, but this is not necessary in all cases.

Experienced When Awake:

- A person complaining of being unable to positively interact with their spouse
- Feelings of extreme hatred towards their spouse

---

[95] Reported Al-Bukhari and Muslim

- Sexual problems such as incompletion of sexual intercourse
- Someone may find it difficult to marry although there would be no obvious indication as to why they cannot.
- Inability to reconcile a marriage (a person's family may also be affected by magic in this scenario)

One of the biggest indications of magic is finding strange objects which is used in the magic:

- Taweez
- Knotted strings, electrical wires or clothing
- Jewelry chains
- Beads
- Strange shaped stones
- Unusual dust or powder such as flour scattered inside or outside the home
- Pins and needles that are poked into the furniture or around the home
- Padlocks, safety pins, bottles, jars
- Holes that have been cut out of one's garments
- Clothes that have been missing and then found again
- Finding clothes that have been stained with the likes of blood
- Finding strange scary objects in hidden places of the house
- Foul odors in places of the home
- Symbols carved inside or outside the home
- Seeing water or liquid sprinkled outside the home by the doorway or over the doorstep
- Broken eggs on the doorstep
- Cats or birds that have been slaughtered
- Nails that have been nailed into the door

Individuals One Might Suspect of Performing Magic

One of the biggest drives for someone doing magic is envy. The second biggest drive is for revenge. The third one is to have control over someone or a particular situation. The fourth drive one might perform magic is for love or obsession. Before we can accuse anyone, there has to be grounds for this suspicion. It cannot be baseless or out of hate, frustration or jealousy to the individual that one might suspect. If one suspects the person of doing magic, he or she still has to prove it with evidence. Seeing the person in a dream is not enough evidence. One of the strongest indications one is capable of doing magic is that they go to magicians and there are reliable just witnesses that see the person go to magician or they themselves practice magic or learn from magicians. We do not take rumors as evidences. We need evidence and facts to confront the person who has done magic and tell them to stop doing magic.

- Receiving threats from close family members, neighbors, coworkers, business partners, or acquaintances
- Some threats may include that an individual will not get married or get a job or threats that one will be separated from their children, husband/wife, etc. and then finding those threats come to pass

Symptoms Within A Person Afflicted by Magic:

- Being extremely volatile (i.e. extreme mood swings)
- Always changing plans (i.e. indecisiveness)
- Anger occurring for small things
- Crying for no reason
- Slipping away or staying away from Deen
- No focus in prayer

- Abandoning the Qur'an
- Tendency towards sins
- Eyes appearing as if one has been taking drugs
- Nausea or vomiting
- Blood pouring out of the mouth without a medical reason
- Continuous bleeding for women
- Repeated miscarriages
- Divorce and re-marrying between a husband and wife for no reason
- Constant headaches and feeling pain in the stomach
- Wanting to vomit when going to the sea, when wind is blowing or walking by graves

Going to Deviant "Healers" and Soothsayers

Going to these individuals is very dangerous in this life and in the next. Usually the magician will inform the individual of the unseen or perform a magic trick to impress and gain the client's trust. In return, the magician might give the client paper, water, foods to eat and drink and bathe from as part of a magic ritual. Below are just some of the many things magicians might have a person do.

- Going to a magician and drinking their water
- Inhaling a magician's Bukhoor (i.e. incense)
- Being given a certain garment to wear with a certain color
- Being given amulets to wear
- Being given amulets, taweez, or strange objects to hang around the house
- Being told slaughter animals
- Being told to do bizarre things like eat insects or forbidden foods

- Being told to perform strange un-Islamic rituals such as staying in a dark room for 40 days
- Being told to hammer nails in the corner of the rooms
- Being told to read words or poems that do not make sense or where the meaning is unknown
- Placing food outside the homes

Treatment Plan for Black Magic (Sihr)

If the magician is known, he must be confronted and told to stop what he is doing. Second, look for the magic around the home and destroy it if found. Third, vomit the magic if it has been digested. It is good to detox the body on a regular basis if magic was ingested. Hijama is highly recommended in this situation.

If you suspect you have been definitely afflicted by magic, then you can follow the program below:

1. Recite Surah Al-Baqarah once daily (two or three times a day if possible). For those that struggle with the recitation itself or with difficulty completing the recitation during one session, it is advised to listen to an audio recitation and put your finger on the words of the Mushaf following the reciter. This might be a difficult habit to start and maintain but it is well worth the efforts as Surah Al-Baqarah is extremely powerful in fighting magic.

2. Recite Surah Al-Falaq throughout the day (even while doing chores, shopping, etc). This is one of the smallest chapters of the Qur'an which most Muslims have memorized from a young age. If you find it difficult to constantly recite Surah Al-Falaq, then I advise you to listen to it multiple times throughout the day at the very least.

3. Recite the following verse frequently: *"Sorcery, Allah will surely make it of no effect"* [Interpretation of Surah Yunus 10:81]. A simpler way to remember it is "magic, Allah will destroy it." Magic does not have an effect except by Allah's permission so call upon Him.

4. Listen to the Black Magic Ruqya audio on https://alruqya.com/sound/.

5. In addition to listening to the Ruqya audio, one should listen to the audio specific to the problem. For example, if one is unable to have children or is going towards divorce, then they should listen to the audios of Talaq (divorce) and the womb. You can find the audios on our website: https://alruqya.com/sound/.

6. Keep in mind that in the beginning, you may not know where the magic is or what type of Jinn you have. However, once you start doing Ruqya and continue to make a lot of Du'a to Allah, things will become much more apparent. During the course of the treatment program, one may be guided by a dream regarding the location of the magic. Examples are if you see mountains in your dreams or if you react to the verses of Ifrit during your Ruqya, then you should listen to the Ruqya audio of mountains in addition to the black magic audio. Likewise, you should listen to the Ruqya audio of the ocean if you see dreams containing different bodies of water or listen to the Ruqya audio of the birds if you see birds in your dreams, etc.

7. Daily words of remembrance for the morning and evening (Adkhaar). This is very important and cannot be stressed enough.

NOTE: If one has been afflicted with magic without Jinn possession, then they should just carry out the above program.

For those afflicted with both Jinn possession and black magic, then in addition to the above, the following should be adhered to:

1. Listen to the Ruqya audio of Advice to the Jinn (Naseeha). This is a great reminder to the Jinn especially those that are arrogant, stubborn, and violent Jinn.

2. Listen to the Ruqya audio of fire (Harq) which is a reminder to the Jinn that they will be punished on the Day of Judgement for oppressing the individual.

3. Listen to the Ruqya audio of destruction (Tadmeer) praying to Allah that He will cause them destruction.

4. Listen to the Ruqya audio of the graveyard. Many Jinn come from the graveyard which magicians use to bury their magic etc. You can also listen to the audios of the planets, sea, birds, and mountains depending on the type of magic that has been done to you.

5. Aayat Al-Kursi audio while sleeping anywhere from 30 minutes to all night depending on the severity of the individual's case. This is the most powerful verse in the Qur'an.

Chapter 18

Jinn Possession

It is from the consensus of Ahl al-Sunnah wal-Jama'ah and by real-life encounters witnessed around the world that Jinn possession is real and has a harmful effect on all aspects of life.

$$\text{ٱلَّذِينَ يَأْكُلُونَ ٱلرِّبَوٰاْ لَا يَقُومُونَ إِلَّا كَمَا يَقُومُ ٱلَّذِى يَتَخَبَّطُهُ ٱلشَّيْطَٰنُ مِنَ ٱلْمَسِّ}$$

"Those who eat Riba [usury] will not stand (on the Day of Resurrection) except like the standing of a person beaten by Shaytan leading him to insanity" [Interpretation of Surah Al-Baqarah 2:275].

Abu Saeed al-Khudri reported that the Messenger of Allah (ﷺ) said: "If any of you yawns, let him cover his mouth lest the Shaytaan enter."[96]

---

[96] Abu Dawud

Anas reported Allah's Messenger as saying, "The devil flows in a man like his blood."[97]

Reasons for Jinn Possession

- Lust: Jinn and mankind can take pleasure from one another just as a man and woman would take pleasure with one another in their everyday interactions. It is not just limited to sexual interactions or to just male to female. Sheikh Al-Islam Ibn Taymiyyah even spoke about this and has mentioned it in his book *Majmoo Al-Fatawa*. When people take their clothes off without saying Bismillah, they make themselves vulnerable to the lustful Jinn. If an individual is vain in terms of their showing off their beauty or beautifying themselves in front of the mirror without mentioning Allah's name or looking at oneself in the mirror without saying the supplication that is prescribed in the Sunnah, they are prone to an attack. Indulging in lustful books and other materials, looking at indecent materials, fantasizing lustful thoughts with an imaginary individual or someone that one knows makes one prone to the lustful Jinn.
- Revenge: If a person hurts a Jinn unintentionally such as by putting water somewhere outside, jumping from a high place, throwing hot water or liquid outside at night, urinating in the bushes or in an insect hole, throwing stones in a body of water, throwing objects at cats, dogs, snakes etc. or if a person unintentionally kills a Jinn, then the individual is prone to an attack.
- Evil Eye: The envious person attracts devils around them. When the envious person looks with admiration or with envy or with hate, the Jinn can potentially

---

[97] Reported by Bukhari and Muslim

attack the person who is being looked at. Allah knows best.

- Magic: Individuals who read books on magic, who call upon the devils or play with ouji boards, tarot cards, do cup reading, visit deviant spiritual healers etc. are prone to possession if they are not already possessed.
- Purely mischievous from the part of the Jinn: The Jinn love evil and encourage evil and disobedience in human beings even if they do not benefit from it as the Jinn love to spread corruption in the land.
- Somebody who turns away from the remembrance of Allah: A person who is not constantly remembering Allah is not protected and is open to an attack at any time.
- Visiting certain places: Individuals who visit locations and events where trances are done, rituals are practiced, idols are worshipped are prone to an attack. Visiting places such as graveyards or visiting palm readers, tarot card readers shamans who give clients mushrooms to hallucinate etc. will also make an individual vulnerable to possession.

Types of Possession

- Full possession: Jinn takes full control of the person/ the person does not remember what happened
- Possession of Jinn that's passing by: possession that happens at a particular time only – e.g. when somebody is asleep he feels someone pressing down on his chest.
- Partial possession: Jinn residing in a particular part of the body which results in heaviness or pain in parts of the body or organ which can result in illnesses

- Half/half Possession: when the person is awake/conscious, and the Jinn is present as well. This is confusing for a person who is possessed.

Signs and Symptoms

The signs and symptoms of Jinn possession can be of a physical, behavioral or psychological nature. There are different times when the signs become apparent. There are signs when one is asleep and signs when one is awake. Raqis have researched and gathered evidence throughout many years regarding the signs and symptoms of Jinn possession from the Qur'an and Sunnah and from their experiences. This is not something new and there are evidences in many hadiths some of which we have already mentioned such as the hadith of Safa' (evil eye of the Jinn) and the hadith of the children of Jafar who suffered from the Evil Eye.

Signs in Dreams

> Jabir reported Allah's Messenger (ﷺ) as saying: There came to him (the Holy Prophet) a desert Arab and said: I saw in a dream that I had been beheaded and I had been following it (the severed head). Allah's Messenger (ﷺ) reprimanded him saying: Do not inform about the vain sporting of devil with you during the night.

The above hadith is evidence that the Shayateen of the Jinn can attack an individual in his dreams. Dreams from the Shayateen should not be mentioned to others. In this way, the dream will not harm you.

Protection from the Jinn When One Goes to Sleep

> Abu Huraira reported: The Messenger of Allah (ﷺ) entrusted me to protect the charity of Ramadan. Someone came to me and began taking from the food. I took hold of him and I said,

"I will certainly take you to the Messenger of Allah (ﷺ)!" Abu Huraira told the story to the Prophet (ﷺ) and he said, "The man told me that when I go to bed, I should recite the verse of the throne. Allah would appoint a protector with me and no devil would come near to me until morning." The Prophet (ﷺ) said, "He told you the truth, although he is a liar. That was Satan."

These two hadiths serve as evidence that one can get attacked in their sleep and the protection for that is Aayat Al-Kursi and if one was to see a disturbing dream then they should not narrate it to another as mentioned in the hadith. Nevertheless, if one feels this disturbance on a regular basis, there is a possibility that this person is afflicted.

Physical Symptoms

> Narrated 'Ata bin Abi Rabah: Ibn Abbas said to me, "Shall I show you a woman of the people of Paradise?" I said, "Yes." He said, "This black lady came to the Prophet (ﷺ) and said, 'I get attacks of epilepsy and my body becomes uncovered; please invoke Allah for me.' The Prophet (ﷺ) said (to her), 'If you wish, be patient and you will have (enter) Paradise; and if you wish, I will invoke Allah to cure you. She said, 'I will remain patient,' and added, 'but I become uncovered, so please invoke Allah for me that I may not become uncovered.' So he invoked Allah for her."

Narrated by 'Ata: That he had seen Umm Zafar, the tall black lady, at (holding) the curtain of the Ka'ba.

In a version narrated by al-Bazzaar, she said, "I am afraid that the evil one may cause me to become uncovered." Al-Haafiz Ibn Hajar said: "It may be understood from some of the different versions of the hadith that what Umm Zafar was suffering from was the kind of epilepsy caused by the Jinn and not that which results from dysfunction in the brain."[98]

Convulsions/Epileptic fits could be minor or severe. They can vary in the level of intensity. The above hadith refers to Jinn possession and not a chemical imbalance in the brain.

Disturbance in the Prayer

> It was narrated that 'Uthman ibn Abul-'As said: "When the Messenger of Allah (ﷺ) appointed me as governor of Ta'if, I began to get confused during my prayer, until I no longer knew what I was doing. When I noticed that, I travelled to the Messenger of Allah (ﷺ), and he said: 'The son of Abul-'As?' I said: 'Yes, O Messenger of Allah.' He said: 'What brings you here?' He said: 'O Messenger of Allah, I get confused during my prayer, until I do not know what I am doing.' He said: 'That is Satan. Come here.' So I came close to him, and sat upon the front part of my feet then he struck my chest with his hand and put some spittle in my mouth and said: 'Get out, O enemy of Allah!' He did that three times, then he said: 'Get on with your work.'" 'Uthman said: "Indeed, I never felt confused (during my prayer) after that."[99]

When one is in acts of worship and feels he is struggling in that aspect and feels a continuous disturbance then this is a possible indication that the person might be afflicted.

Extreme Anger

> Narrated Sulaiman ibn Surd: While I was sitting in the company of the Prophet, two men abused each other and the face of one of them became red with anger, and his jugular veins swelled (i.e. he became furious). On that the Prophet said, "I know a word, the saying of which will cause him to relax, if he does say it. If he says: 'I seek Refuge with Allah from Satan.'

---

[98] Fath al-Baari
[99] Reported by Ibn Majah, authenticatd by Albanee

then all is anger will go away." Somebody said to him, "The Prophet has said, 'Seek refuge with Allah from Satan.'" The angry man said, "Am I mad?"[100]

Turning Away from the Remembrance of Allah

وَمَن يَعْشُ عَن ذِكْرِ ٱلرَّحْمَٰنِ نُقَيِّضْ لَهُ شَيْطَٰنًا فَهُوَ لَهُ قَرِينٌ

"And whoever is blinded from remembrance of the Most Merciful - We appoint for him a devil, and he is to him a companion."
[Interpretation of Surah Az-Zukhruf 43:36].

There are many hadiths and verses of the Qur'an that allude to the understanding that the Shayateen attack mankind.

Signs When Asleep

- Nightmares
- Dreams of a sexual nature
- Seeing unpleasant dreams – figures and animals
- Sleep walking
- Unusual behavior when asleep
- Sleep Paralysis
- Disturbed sleep

Signs When Awake

- Convulsions/seizures without medical reason
- Paralysis of the limbs
- Extreme anger
- Erratic behavior could be at different levels such as mood swings, split personality
- Turning away from the remembrance of Allah

---

[100] Reported by Bukhari

- Fighting against the commands of Allah
- Struggling with acts of worship

Signs & Symptoms During Ruqya

When performing Ruqya on the one who is afflicted, certain signs and symptoms become more apparent and clearer but not in all cases and usually not all straight away.

- Pain around the body
- Movement felt in the body
- Heat around the body
- Hot or cold flushes
- Feeling heavy
- Feeling dizzy
- Feeling tired and need to sleep
- Some feel like they need to stretch and yawn when they have had enough sleep the night before
- Some would have hatred towards the therapist
- Some will be abusive and angry
- Staring at the Raqi in a very angry manner
- Looking away, no eye contact, looking to the corners of the room
- Some will threaten Raqis indirectly
- Some will fall to the ground and have a convulsion
- Some would be stone cold or display unusual behavior
- Some would just start coughing
- The sign could be very small such as raising a hand or finger
- Change in the pattern of breathing
- Twitching in the body
- Muscle spasms
- Cramps

These signs can be found in people who suffer from evil eye and black magic as Jinn can possess through those. Please note that these signs only show when the Ruqya is performed on the individual and they increase as more Qur'an is recited or the signs can totally go away which is a good thing. And Allah knows best.

Signs of Jinn Possession Found in the Home

As well as possessing the body of a person, the Jinn can also interfere and intimidate the person around the house.

- Objects move around seemingly by themselves
- Objects may disappear and not be found again
- Objects may disappear and be found in another location
- Objects may disappear and later be found where they originally were
- Objects may come from nowhere
- Objects fly around as if they were thrown from unseen hands
- Knocking, banging, pounding or thuds may be heard throughout the house or in just one room
- Religious articles disappear or are destroyed or may also be desecrated
- Growling, snarling, or hissing may be heard but the source cannot be located
- People may hear voices when no one is present.
- People will often hear their name called only to find that no one is around. Sometimes, a couple will each think they heard the other call to them
- There may be scratching sounds heard without an obvious source
- There may be foul odors that have no verifiable source that may come and go

- Heavy furniture may move on its own
- Doors and drawers may open and close on their own
- Levitation of objects or people
- Electrical appliances or lights may turn on or off
- Spontaneous fires may start up
- Glass may break for no reason
- Sounds of glass breaking may be heard but there is no evidence of it happening
- There may be sudden temperature changes, up and down although it is usually down. These can be recorded on a thermometer.
- There may be a sensation of wind or a light breeze blowing even with the windows being closed.
- Odd lights may be seen; it may shoot around a room.
- Lights will go off or not come on when turned on.
- There may be sightings of people or dark shadows that may or may not have form.
- Odd-looking creatures may be seen
- Reptiles, insects, or rodent invasion in the home
- People may have a feeling of being watched or that they are not alone.
- Any talk about Allah and Islam/religion may cause an outbreak of paranormal activity.
- Activity starts up when reciting and listening to Qur'an, Adhaan and making Du'a etc.
- Apparent retaliation if a Raqi has been to the home
- Apparent retaliation after some attempt to stop the activity

The following signs can occur both at home and outside the home:
- Animals may become spooked and stay away from the targeted person altogether.

- Animals may growl at something they see but you do not.

These signs can be found in people who suffer from evil eye and black magic as Jinn can possess through them.

Treatment Program for Jinn Possession in the Home

Recite Surah Al-Baqarah once daily (two or three times a day if possible). For those that struggle with the recitation itself or with difficulty completing the recitation during one session, it is advised to listen to an audio recitation and put your finger on the words of the Mushaf following the reciter. This might be a difficult habit to start and maintain but it is well worth the efforts as Surah Al-Baqarah is extremely powerful in fighting the Jinn. Recite Surah As-Saffat and Surah Al-Jinn in the home. In addition, please refer to chapter of Preparing the Home for Ruqya.

Treatment Program for Jinn Possession & Lustful Jinn

It is very common for a Jinni when possessing the individual to become infatuated and obsessive over the person which can cause the individual a lot of harm.

1. Be close to Allah by reciting the Qur'an every day, do good deeds often, fast, keep the tongue moist with the remembrance of Allah, make Tawba, etc.

2. Adhere to the Ruqya program you have put together yourself or given in this book or by a Raqi and be consistent with it.

3. Find what the Jinni's weaknesses are and its dislikes.

4. Keep the home clean and spray it with Ruqya water, play the Qur'an, get rid of anything that is forbidden such as pictures, statues and images, playing music, musical instrument, or watching anything indecent, etc.

5. Use black seed oil, olive oil, asafetida oil, Ruqya water, and other supplements.

6. Have hijama done regularly, drink Zamzam water, and eat dates.

7. For a married couple, one's spouse is key to the treatment program. It is important to please each other, to show more love and affection, to try not to be angry with each other and to make sure there is more harmony in the home.

8. Give more hugs and kisses to children/family as the Jinn Aashiq dislikes this.

9. Burn black seeds and frankincense over a coal to the private part by standing over the smoke or carefully steam the private part. (Depends on the type of Jinn and this is where profiling the Jinn becomes important to know the likes and dislikes of the particular Jinn).

10. Use black musk or

11. Use asafetida oil or

12. Frankincense oil

13. Find the location of the Jinn in the body and treat it accordingly using a tens machine or a deep heat cream or tiger rub or pure cinnamon essential oil or cold pressed cinnamon oil.

14. Using an MP3 player or Bluetooth portable speaker, apply the sound of the Qur'an in the area. You can take a portable

speaker and place it on your stomach, back, neck, thigh, etc.

15. Climax during intimacy if married. This is extremely important as Aashiqs hate this and use lack of climax to cause friction in marriage and in some cases even divorce. A couple should be open to one another and discuss this freely and comfortably to come to a good outcome for both as Jinn use this as a leverage against couples.

16. Do not pay too much attention to the Jinn. They can play with the individual by showing them dreams. This should be ignored as the Jinn dislikes being ignored.

17. Do not be depressed and make a greater effort to continue to live life normally and to remain productive.

18. Do not look at oneself admiringly and always make Du'a when looking in the mirror, and say "Bismillah" before removing clothing.

19. If the individual finds themselves obsessively looking at themselves in the mirror too much, they should spray the mirror with Ruqya water or cover the mirror.

20. To listen to the <u>Ruqya audios</u> on our website.

   a. Number 4: Sihr (black magic) or Number 3: Evil Eye Ruqya audio

   b. Number 7: Harq (burning) Ruqya audio

   c. Number 9: Zina (adultery) Ruqya audio

21. To listen/recite Surah An-Noor and Surah Yusuf.

22. Last but not least, make Du'a! Spend at least an hour dedicating time to make Du'a for Allah to remove the affliction, to forgive you, and to grant you patience. Du'a is

the greatest weapon of the believer. Do not underestimate its power.

Chapter 19

Ruqya Audios & Their Usage

Audio #1: Surah Al-Baqarah: Surah Baqarah is one of the most powerful chapters in the Qur'an as it contains some of the most powerful verses such as the verse of the Throne. Magicians cannot compete with it. It drives away the devils from the home. It brings blessings to all aspects of your life: your health, your wealth, etc. It will intercede for you on the Day of Judgement. Surah Baqarah is extremely beneficial if one reads it every day. This audio is used as a means against all afflictions and is a cause for many benefits in this life and the next.

Audio #2: General Ruqyah: This audio is a general ruqya for black magic, evil eye and Jinn possession. Some people might not react to these verses as most Jinn have heard it and become accustomed to it.

Audio #3: Treatment against Evil Eye: These contain verses for evil eye and envy. The evil eye affects everything. This audio is beneficial for individuals suffering from evil eye (Ayn) the audio is followed by supplications against the evil eye.

Audio #4: Treatment against Black Magic: This audio is beneficial for individuals suffering from black magic, the audio is followed by supplications against black magic.

Audio #5: Treatment against Evil Eye/Black Magic on ilm (Knowledge): This audio is beneficial for individuals who are suffering from evil eye or black magic against their knowledge.

Audio #6: Treatment for Advice (Naseeha): This audio is beneficial for individuals suffering from Jinn possession. The audio consists of giving the Jinn advice and asking them to fear Allah (SWT) and to return back to the worship of their lord.

Audio #7: Treatment for Burning (Harq): This audio is a combination of verses that are known to be powerful against punishing the Jinn. The verses used are intended towards burning the stubborn ones in particular from amongst the Jinn.

Audio #8: Treatment for Healing (Shifa): This audio is for general health complaints. The Qur'an is a healing for all diseases as Allah (SWT) says: "And We send down of the Qur'an that which is a healing and a mercy for the believers, but it does not increase the wrongdoers except in loss." (Al-Isra:82)

Audio #9: Treatment against Adultery/Fornication (Zina): This ruqya audio is for people suffering from excessive desires and Jinn aashiq (lustful Jinn).

Audio #10: Summarized Ruqya (Mokhtasar): This audio is a summarised ruqya for black magic, evil eye & Jinn possession.

Audio #11: Treatment for Divorce (Talaq): This audio contains verses from the Qur'an which tackle the issue of divorce and afflictions in the wombs caused by evil eye, black magic or Jinn possession.

Audio #12: Treatment for Destruction (Tadmeer): This audio is intended for those who receive a lot of violence in their dreams, get attacked in their dreams or see visions of violence. This audio is NOT to be listened to while driving.

Audio #13: Surah Al-Falaq & Surah An-Naas: This audio is powerful against black magic, evil eye and Jinn possession

Audio #14: Aayat-Al-Kursi: Aayat Al-Kursi is the most powerful Ayah in the Qur'an and its effects on punishing the evil ones from the Shayateen are great.

Audio #15: Prayers upon the Prophet (ﷺ): This audio is continual prayers upon the Prophet (ﷺ).

Audio #16: Jews (Yahood): This audio is to be used to treat Jewish Jinn, black magic or evil eye.

Audio #17: Christians (Nasaarah): This audio is used to treat the effects of Christian Jinn possession, black magic or evil eye.

Audio #18: Surah As-Saffat: This audio is Surah As-Saffaat in full which is very effective against Jinn possession.

Audio #19: Surah Al-Jinn: This audio is Surah Al-Jinn in full, which is very effective against Jinn possession.

Audio #20: Surah Yaseen: This audio is Surah Yaseen in full, which serves as a reminder to both man and Jinn. Initially, there are many reminders of the hereafter.

Audio #21: Live recording of a Ruqya session only with headphones: This is a live recording of one of Shaykh Khalid Al-Hibshi's sessions.

Audio #22: Birds (At-Tuyuur): This audio is effective against the flying type of Jinn. It is also effective against magic that has been used on birds or attached to birds or their wings.

Audio #23: Provisions (Rizq): This audio is effective against blockages in wealth, whether it is through black magic, evil eye or Jinn possession.

Audio #24: Mountains (Al-Jibaal): This audio is effective against Jinn from the mountains or black magic which has been placed on the mountains.

Audio #25: Guidance & Repentance: This audio contains verses that serve as a reminder to man and Jinn alike. It is aimed for their guidance and to encourage repentance towards their creator, Allah (SWT).

Chapter 20

Supplements & Their Usage

Olive Oil: "Lit from a blessed tree, neither of the East nor of the west…" The olive tree was mentioned in the Qur'an twice as being a blessed tree. The Prophet (ﷺ) also said, "Eat from the olive oil and anoint yourselves with it, because it comes from a blessed tree." This oil contains chlorophyll which is a powerful antioxidant and powerful blood purifier causing Sihr or Ayn to be removed from the veins. The ideal oil is organic, raw and unprocessed.

Rue Oil: Ruta graveolens is most commonly known as rue, common rue or herb of grace or Sudhab in Arabic. It is used as a small amount to drink daily and to take a bath with or to mix the oil with olive oil to rub on the body. Rue oil is known to be effective and shown positive results in the calming or prevention of epileptic tremors/fits caused by Jinn.

Black Seed Oil: Its scientific name is Nigella Sativa. The black seeds should be organic. The Prophet (ﷺ) said, regarding black seeds, "It is a cure from every illness."[101] The color of the oil is

---

[101] Reported by Bukhari and Muslim

black, demonstrating the strength and purity of the oil. The Prophet (ﷺ) said, about black seed oil, "in black seed is a cure for every disease except death."

Frankincense Oil: This oil is beneficial for Ayn. It has a calmative effect which prevents a person from getting nervous disorders, anxiety associated with Ayn. Frankincense oil is suitable for internal consumption as it is well known for treating various different symptoms such as evil eye, envy, digestion issues, anxiety, arthritis, inflammation, and asthma along with many other symptoms. It is also used to prevent harm from the Shayateen.
How to use: You can consume it or apply directly over your head and chest.

Indian Costus Oil: This oil is particularly beneficial for hurting or even killing Jinn that has settled in the brain. You can use this oil externally or sniff it through the nose. Lie down on your back with the head tilted back and sniff it. If it's a powder, then you can mix it with ruqyah water or olive oil and sniff it. This should cause the patient to sneeze any sickness or the Jinn to burn or flee. The Prophet (ﷺ) said, "Use 'Oud al-Hindi because it contains seven types of cures, if it is sniffed by the one having throat trouble, and is put inside the mouth of one suffering from pleurisy."

Asafoetida Oil: This oil helps with Jinn Aashiqs (lustful demons) as they do not like the smell. Use it in the bath as a soak or rub it on the private parts.

Sidr Leaves: The best sidr leaves are wild, organic and grown naturally without traditional farm practices. Sidr is very beneficial in curing sihr especially issues related to male impotency. Imam Ibn Hajar (may Allah have mercy upon him reported in his book Al-Fath from Wahb Ibn Munaabbih (may

Allah have mercy upon him) the way of using Sidr leaves (Lotus jujube) as a remedy to be rid of bewitchment. He said, "One should take seven leaves of green Lotus jujube, grind them between two stones, put the stones and the leaves in some water, then take out the two stones. Having done so, he should recite the verse of the Kursi (Chair) [Qur'an 2:255] and the last three chapters of the Qur'an [Qur'an 112,113,114]" Al-Lalkaii said that Mohamed ibn Othman related that Said bin Mohamed Al-Hanat stated: "Ishaq ibn Abi Israel said ' I heard Sufyan say that Sulayman ibn Omaya (Sheikh of Thaqif) ibn Masoud heard Aisha advise a woman to use Sidr and water to wash the traces of magic (Sharh Usul Itiqad Ahl Al-Sunnah wa Al-Jamaa -7/1288). His Honor, Sheikh Abdulaziz bin Abdullah bin Baz, (May Allah have Mercy on Him) said that the cure of magic after its affliction is beneficial, Allah Willing. However, its benefit is not only confined to men who cannot have intercourse with his wives but also includes those afflicted with epilepsy, evil eye and magic in general (used for washing only).

Instructions for use: Grind seven leaves and place the leaves in a bucket of ruqyah water.

For more supplements & their benefits, please visit https://www.ruqyainlondon.com/.

Chapter 21

Ruqya Verses

I have included the Arabic transliteration for each type of treatment. Arabic transliteration is not something you should rely on. I have included it to help you with the reading, but I strongly encourage you to learn and practice Arabic. You can go online or use apps to help you read and pronounce the Arabic verses.

General Ruqya Verses

ايآت الرقية الشرعية

أعوذ بالله السميع العليم من الشيطان الرجيم

A'udhu Billahi min ash shaytaani'r rajeem

I seek refuge with Allah from Shaytan the accursed

بِسْمِ اللَّهِ الرَّحْمَٰنِ الرَّحِيمِ

Bismi Allahi alrrahmani alrraheemi

In the name of Allah, the Entirely Merciful, the Especially Merciful

❁ بِسْمِ اللَّهِ الرَّحْمَٰنِ الرَّحِيمِ ﴿١﴾ الْحَمْدُ لِلَّهِ رَبِّ الْعَالَمِينَ ﴿٢﴾ الرَّحْمَٰنِ الرَّحِيمِ ﴿٣﴾ مَالِكِ يَوْمِ الدِّينِ ﴿٤﴾ إِيَّاكَ نَعْبُدُ وَإِيَّاكَ نَسْتَعِينُ ﴿٥﴾ اهْدِنَا الصِّرَاطَ الْمُسْتَقِيمَ ﴿٦﴾ صِرَاطَ الَّذِينَ أَنْعَمْتَ عَلَيْهِمْ غَيْرِ الْمَغْضُوبِ عَلَيْهِمْ وَلَا الضَّالِّينَ   [الفاتحة: 1-7]

Bismi Allahi alrrahmani alrraheemi (1) Alhamdu lillahi rabbi alAAalameena (2) Alrrahmani alrraheemi (3) Maliki yawmi alddeeni (4) Iyyaka naAAbudu waiyyaka nastaAAeenu (5) Ihdina alssirata almustaqeema (6) Sirata allatheena anAAamta AAalayhim ghayri almaghdoobi AAalayhim wala alddalleena (7)

In the name of Allah, the Entirely Merciful, the Especially Merciful. (1) [All] praise is [due] to Allah, Lord of the worlds - (2) The Entirely Merciful, the Especially Merciful, (3) Sovereign of the Day of Recompense. (4) It is You we worship and You we ask for help. (5) Guide us to the straight path - (6) The path of those upon whom You have bestowed favour, not of those who have evoked [Your] anger or of those who are astray. (7)

108

بِسْمِ اللهِ الرَّحْمٰنِ الرَّحِيمِ

Bismi Allahi alrrahmani alrraheemi

In the name of Allah, the Entirely Merciful, the Especially Merciful

الم ﴿١﴾ ذَٰلِكَ الْكِتَابُ لَا رَيْبَ ۛ فِيهِ ۛ هُدًى لِّلْمُتَّقِينَ ﴿٢﴾ الَّذِينَ يُؤْمِنُونَ بِالْغَيْبِ وَيُقِيمُونَ الصَّلَاةَ وَمِمَّا رَزَقْنَاهُمْ يُنفِقُونَ ﴿٣﴾ وَالَّذِينَ يُؤْمِنُونَ بِمَا أُنزِلَ إِلَيْكَ وَمَا أُنزِلَ مِن قَبْلِكَ وَبِالْآخِرَةِ هُمْ يُوقِنُونَ ﴿٤﴾ أُولَٰئِكَ عَلَىٰ هُدًى مِّن رَّبِّهِمْ ۖ وَأُولَٰئِكَ هُمُ الْمُفْلِحُونَ ﴿٥﴾ [البقرة: 1-5]

Aliflammeem (1) Thalika alkitabu la rayba feehi hudan lilmuttaqeena (2) Allatheena yuminoona bialghaybi wayuqeemoona alssalata wamimma razaqnahum yunfiqoona (3) Waallatheena yuminoona bima onzila ilayka wama onzila min qablika wabialakhirati hum yooqinoona (4) Olaika AAala hudan min rabbihim waolaika humu almuflihoona (5)

Alif, Lam, Meem. (1) This is the Book about which there is no doubt, a guidance for those conscious of Allah - (2) Who believe in the unseen, establish prayer, and spend out of what We have provided for them, (3) And who believe in what has been revealed to you, [O Muhammad], and what was revealed before you, and of the Hereafter they are certain [in faith]. (4) Those are upon [right] guidance from their Lord, and it is those who are the successful. (5)

وَإِلَٰهُكُمْ إِلَٰهٌ وَاحِدٌ ۖ لَّا إِلَٰهَ إِلَّا هُوَ الرَّحْمَٰنُ الرَّحِيمُ ﴿١٦٣﴾ إِنَّ فِي خَلْقِ السَّمَاوَاتِ وَالْأَرْضِ وَاخْتِلَافِ اللَّيْلِ وَالنَّهَارِ وَالْفُلْكِ الَّتِي تَجْرِي فِي الْبَحْرِ بِمَا يَنفَعُ النَّاسَ وَمَا أَنزَلَ اللَّهُ مِنَ السَّمَاءِ مِن مَّاءٍ فَأَحْيَا بِهِ الْأَرْضَ بَعْدَ مَوْتِهَا وَبَثَّ فِيهَا مِن كُلِّ دَابَّةٍ وَتَصْرِيفِ الرِّيَاحِ وَالسَّحَابِ الْمُسَخَّرِ بَيْنَ السَّمَاءِ وَالْأَرْضِ لَآيَاتٍ لِّقَوْمٍ يَعْقِلُونَ ﴿١٦٤﴾ [البقرة: 163-164]

Wailahukum ilahun wahidun la ilaha illa huwa alrrahmanu alrraheemu (163) Inna fee khalqi alssamawati waalardi waikhtilafi allayli waalnnahari waalfulki allatee tajree fee albahri bima yanfaAAu alnnasa wama anzala Allahu mina alssamai min main faahya bihi alarda baAAda mawtiha wabaththa feeha min kulli dabbatin watasreefi alrriyahi waalssahabi almusakhkhari bayna alssamai waalardi laayatin liqawmin yaAAqiloona (164)

And your god is one God. There is no deity [worthy of worship] except Him, the Entirely Merciful, the Especially Merciful. (163) Indeed, in the creation of the heavens and earth, and the alternation of the night and the day, and the [great] ships which sail through the sea with that which benefits people, and what Allah has sent down from the heavens of rain, giving life thereby to the earth after its lifelessness and dispersing therein every [kind of] moving creature, and [His] directing of the winds and the clouds controlled between the heaven and the earth are signs for a people who use reason. (164)

اللَّهُ لَا إِلَٰهَ إِلَّا هُوَ الْحَيُّ الْقَيُّومُ ۚ لَا تَأْخُذُهُ سِنَةٌ وَلَا نَوْمٌ ۚ لَّهُ مَا فِي السَّمَاوَاتِ وَمَا فِي الْأَرْضِ ۗ مَن ذَا الَّذِي يَشْفَعُ عِندَهُ إِلَّا بِإِذْنِهِ ۚ يَعْلَمُ مَا بَيْنَ أَيْدِيهِمْ وَمَا خَلْفَهُمْ ۖ وَلَا يُحِيطُونَ بِشَيْءٍ مِّنْ عِلْمِهِ إِلَّا بِمَا شَاءَ ۚ وَسِعَ كُرْسِيُّهُ السَّمَاوَاتِ وَالْأَرْضَ ۖ وَلَا يَئُودُهُ حِفْظُهُمَا ۚ وَهُوَ الْعَلِيُّ الْعَظِيمُ ﴿٢٥٥﴾ [البقرة: 255]

Allahu la ilaha illa huwa alhayyu alqayyoomu la takhuthuhu sinatun wala nawmun lahu ma fee alssamawati wama fee alardi man tha allathee yashfaAAu AAindahu illa biithnihi yaAAlamu ma bayna aydeehim wama khalfahum wala yuheetoona bishayin min AAilmihi illa bima shaa wasiAAa kursiyyuhu alssamawati waalarda wala yaooduhu hifthuhuma wahuwa alAAaliyyu alAAatheemu (255)

Allah - there is no deity except Him, the Ever-Living, the Sustainer of [all] existence. Neither drowsiness overtakes Him nor sleep. To Him belongs whatever is in the heavens and whatever is on the earth. Who is it that can intercede with Him except by His permission? He knows what is [presently] before them and what will be after them, and they encompass not a thing of His knowledge except for what He wills. His Kursi extends over the heavens and the earth, and their preservation tires Him not. And He is the Most High, the Most Great. (255)

111

آمَنَ الرَّسُولُ بِمَا أُنزِلَ إِلَيْهِ مِن رَّبِّهِ وَالْمُؤْمِنُونَ ۚ كُلٌّ آمَنَ بِاللَّهِ وَمَلَائِكَتِهِ وَكُتُبِهِ وَرُسُلِهِ لَا نُفَرِّقُ بَيْنَ أَحَدٍ مِّن رُّسُلِهِ ۚ وَقَالُوا سَمِعْنَا وَأَطَعْنَا ۖ غُفْرَانَكَ رَبَّنَا وَإِلَيْكَ الْمَصِيرُ

﴿٢٨٥﴾ لَا يُكَلِّفُ اللَّهُ نَفْسًا إِلَّا وُسْعَهَا ۚ لَهَا مَا كَسَبَتْ وَعَلَيْهَا مَا اكْتَسَبَتْ ۗ رَبَّنَا لَا تُؤَاخِذْنَا إِن نَّسِينَا أَوْ أَخْطَأْنَا ۚ رَبَّنَا وَلَا تَحْمِلْ عَلَيْنَا إِصْرًا كَمَا حَمَلْتَهُ عَلَى الَّذِينَ مِن قَبْلِنَا ۚ رَبَّنَا وَلَا تُحَمِّلْنَا مَا لَا طَاقَةَ لَنَا بِهِ ۖ وَاعْفُ عَنَّا وَاغْفِرْ لَنَا وَارْحَمْنَا ۚ أَنتَ مَوْلَانَا فَانصُرْنَا عَلَى الْقَوْمِ الْكَافِرِينَ ﴿٢٨٦﴾ [البقرة: 285- 286]

Amana alrrasoolu bima onzila ilayhi min rabbihi waalmuminoona kullun amana biAllahi wamalaikatihi wakutubihi warusulihi la nufarriqu bayna ahadin min rusulihi waqaloo samiAAna waataAAna ghufranaka rabbana wailayka almaseeru (285) La yukallifu Allahu nafsan illa wusAAaha laha ma kasabat waAAalayha ma iktasabat rabbana la tuakhithna in naseena aw akhtana rabbana wala tahmil AAalayna isran kama hamaltahu AAala allatheena min qablina rabbana wala tuhammilna ma la taqata lana bihi waoAAfu AAanna waighfir lana wairhamna anta mawlana faonsurna AAala alqawmi alkafireena (286)

The Messenger has believed in what was revealed to him from his Lord, and [so have] the believers. All of them have believed in Allah and His angels and His books and His messengers, [saying], "We make no distinction between any of His messengers." And they say, "We hear and we obey. [We seek] Your forgiveness, our Lord, and to You is the [final] destination." (285) Allah does not charge a soul except [with that within] its capacity. It will have [the consequence of] what [good] it has gained, and it will bear [the consequence of] what [evil] it has earned. "Our Lord, do not impose blame upon us if we have forgotten or erred. Our Lord, and lay not upon us a burden like that which You laid upon those before us. Our Lord, and burden us not with that which we have no ability to bear. And pardon us; and forgive us; and have mercy upon us. You are our protector, so give us victory over the disbelieving people." (286)

شَهِدَ اللَّهُ أَنَّهُ لَا إِلَهَ إِلَّا هُوَ وَالْمَلَائِكَةُ وَأُولُو الْعِلْمِ قَائِمًا بِالْقِسْطِ ۚ لَا إِلَهَ إِلَّا هُوَ الْعَزِيزُ الْحَكِيمُ ﴿١٨﴾ [آل عمران: 18]

Shahida Allahu annahu la ilaha illa huwa waalmalaikatu waoloo alAAilmi qaiman bialqisti la ilaha illa huwa alAAazeezu alhakeemu (18)

Allah witnesses that there is no deity except Him, and [so do] the angels and those of knowledge - [that He is] maintaining [creation] in justice. There is no deity except Him, the Exalted in Might, the Wise. (18)

إِنَّ رَبَّكُمُ اللَّهُ الَّذِي خَلَقَ السَّمَاوَاتِ وَالْأَرْضَ فِي سِتَّةِ أَيَّامٍ ثُمَّ اسْتَوَىٰ عَلَى الْعَرْشِ يُغْشِي اللَّيْلَ النَّهَارَ يَطْلُبُهُ حَثِيثًا وَالشَّمْسَ وَالْقَمَرَ وَالنُّجُومَ مُسَخَّرَاتٍ بِأَمْرِهِ ۗ أَلَا لَهُ الْخَلْقُ وَالْأَمْرُ ۗ تَبَارَكَ اللَّهُ رَبُّ الْعَالَمِينَ ﴿٥٤﴾ ادْعُوا رَبَّكُمْ تَضَرُّعًا وَخُفْيَةً ۚ إِنَّهُ لَا يُحِبُّ الْمُعْتَدِينَ ﴿٥٥﴾ وَلَا تُفْسِدُوا فِي الْأَرْضِ بَعْدَ إِصْلَاحِهَا وَادْعُوهُ خَوْفًا وَطَمَعًا ۚ إِنَّ رَحْمَتَ اللَّهِ قَرِيبٌ مِّنَ الْمُحْسِنِينَ ﴿٥٦﴾ [الأعرا: 55-56]

Inna rabbakumu Allahu allathee khalaqa alssamawati waalarda fee sittati ayyamin thumma istawa AAala alAAarshi yughshee allayla alnnahara yatlubuhu hatheethan waalshshamsa waalqamara waalnnujooma musakhkharatin biamrihi ala lahu alkhalqu waalamru tabaraka Allahu rabbu alAAalameena (54) OdAAoo rabbakum tadarruAAan wakhufyatan innahu la yuhibbu almuAAtadeena (55) Wala tufsidoo fee alardi baAAda islahiha waodAAoohu khawfan watamaAAan inna rahmata Allahi qareebun mina almuhsineena (56)

Indeed, your Lord is Allah, who created the heavens and earth in six days and then established Himself above the Throne. He covers the night with the day, [another night] chasing it rapidly; and [He created] the sun, the moon, and the stars, subjected by His command. Unquestionably, His is the creation and the command; blessed is Allah, Lord of the worlds. (54) Call upon your Lord in humility and privately; indeed, He does not like transgressors.

113

(55) And cause not corruption upon the earth after its reformation. And invoke Him in fear and aspiration. Indeed, the mercy of Allah is near to the doers of good. (56)

أَفَحَسِبْتُمْ أَنَّمَا خَلَقْنَاكُمْ عَبَثًا وَأَنَّكُمْ إِلَيْنَا لَا تُرْجَعُونَ ﴿١١٥﴾ فَتَعَالَى اللَّهُ الْمَلِكُ
الْحَقُّ ۖ لَا إِلَٰهَ إِلَّا هُوَ رَبُّ الْعَرْشِ الْكَرِيمِ ﴿١١٦﴾ وَمَن يَدْعُ مَعَ اللَّهِ إِلَٰهًا آخَرَ
لَا بُرْهَانَ لَهُ بِهِ فَإِنَّمَا حِسَابُهُ عِندَ رَبِّهِ ۚ إِنَّهُ لَا يُفْلِحُ الْكَافِرُونَ ﴿١١٧﴾ وَقُل رَّبِّ
اغْفِرْ وَارْحَمْ وَأَنتَ خَيْرُ الرَّاحِمِينَ ﴿١١٨﴾   [المؤمنون: 115-118]

Afahasibtum annama khalaqnakum AAabathan waannakum
ilayna la turjaAAoona (115) FataAAala Allahu almaliku alhaqqu
la ilaha illa huwa rabbu alAAarshi alkareemi (116) Waman
yadAAu maAAa Allahi ilahan akhara la burhana lahu bihi
fainnama hisabuhu AAinda rabbihi innahu la yuflihu alkafiroona
(117) Waqul rabbi ighfir wairham waanta khayru alrrahimeena
(118)

Then did you think that We created you uselessly and that to Us
you would not be returned?" (115) So exalted is Allah, the
Sovereign, the Truth; there is no deity except Him, Lord of the
Noble Throne. (116) And whoever invokes besides Allah another
deity for which he has no proof - then his account is only with his
Lord. Indeed, the disbelievers will not succeed. (117) And, [O
Muhammad], say, "My Lord, forgive and have mercy, and You
are the best of the merciful." (118)

وَالصَّافَّاتِ صَفًّا ﴿١﴾ فَالزَّاجِرَاتِ زَجْرًا ﴿٢﴾ فَالتَّالِيَاتِ ذِكْرًا ﴿٣﴾ إِنَّ إِلَهَكُمْ
لَوَاحِدٌ ﴿٤﴾ رَّبُّ السَّمَاوَاتِ وَالْأَرْضِ وَمَا بَيْنَهُمَا وَرَبُّ الْمَشَارِقِ ﴿٥﴾ إِنَّا زَيَّنَّا
السَّمَاءَ الدُّنْيَا بِزِينَةٍ الْكَوَاكِبِ ﴿٦﴾ وَحِفْظًا مِّن كُلِّ شَيْطَانٍ مَّارِدٍ ﴿٧﴾ لَّا
يَسَّمَّعُونَ إِلَى الْمَلَإِ الْأَعْلَىٰ وَيُقْذَفُونَ مِن كُلِّ جَانِبٍ ﴿٨﴾ دُحُورًا وَلَهُمْ عَذَابٌ
وَاصِبٌ ﴿٩﴾ إِلَّا مَنْ خَطِفَ الْخَطْفَةَ فَأَتْبَعَهُ شِهَابٌ ثَاقِبٌ
﴿١٠﴾   [الصَّافَّات: 10-1]

By those [angels] lined up in rows (1) And those who drive [the
clouds] (2) And those who recite the message, (3) Indeed, your
God is One, (4) Lord of the heavens and the earth and that
between them and Lord of the sunrises. (5) Indeed, We have
adorned the nearest heaven with an adornment of stars (6) And as
protection against every rebellious devil (7) [So] they may not
listen to the exalted assembly [of angels] and are pelted from every
side, (8) Repelled; and for them is a constant punishment,
(9) Except one who snatches [some words] by theft, but they are
pursued by a burning flame, piercing [in brightness]. (10)

Waalssaffati saffan (1) Faalzzajirati zajran (2) Faalttaliyati thikran
(3) Inna ilahakum lawahidun (4) Rabbu alssamawati waalardi
wama baynahuma warabbu almashariqi (5) Inna zayyanna
alssamaa alddunya bizeenatin alkawakibi (6) Wahifthan min kulli
shaytanin maridin (7) La yassammaAAoona ila almalai
alaAAla ayuqthafoona min kulli janibin (8) Duhooran walahum
AAathabun wasibun (9) Illa man khatifa alkhatfata faatbaAAahu
shihabun thaqibun (10)

116

يَا مَعْشَرَ الْجِنِّ وَالْإِنسِ إِنِ اسْتَطَعْتُمْ أَن تَنفُذُوا مِنْ أَقْطَارِ السَّمَاوَاتِ وَالْأَرْضِ فَانفُذُوا ۚ لَا تَنفُذُونَ إِلَّا بِسُلْطَانٍ ﴿٣٣﴾ فَبِأَيِّ آلَاءِ رَبِّكُمَا تُكَذِّبَانِ ﴿٣٤﴾ يُرْسَلُ عَلَيْكُمَا شُوَاظٌ مِّن نَّارٍ وَنُحَاسٌ فَلَا تَنتَصِرَانِ ﴿٣٥﴾ فَبِأَيِّ آلَاءِ رَبِّكُمَا تُكَذِّبَانِ ﴿٣٦﴾ [الرحمن: 36-33]

Ya maAAshara aljinni waalinsi ini istataAAtum an tanfuthoo min aqtari alssamawati waalardi faonfuthoo la tanfuthoona illa bisultanin (33) Fabiayyi alai rabbikuma tukaththibani (34) Yursalu AAalaykuma shuwathun min narin wanuhasun fala tantasirani (35) Fabiayyi alai rabbikuma tukaththibani (36)

O company of Jinn and mankind, if you are able to pass beyond the regions of the heavens and the earth, then pass. You will not pass except by authority [from Allah]. (33) So which of the favors of your Lord would you deny? (34) There will be sent upon you a flame of fire and smoke, and you will not defend yourselves. (35) So which of the favors of your Lord would you deny? (36)

لَوْ أَنْزَلْنَا هَٰذَا الْقُرْآنَ عَلَىٰ جَبَلٍ لَرَأَيْتَهُ خَاشِعًا مُتَصَدِّعًا مِّن خَشْيَةِ اللَّهِ ۚ وَتِلْكَ الْأَمْثَالُ نَضْرِبُهَا لِلنَّاسِ لَعَلَّهُمْ يَتَفَكَّرُونَ ﴿٢١﴾ هُوَ اللَّهُ الَّذِي لَا إِلَٰهَ إِلَّا هُوَ ۖ عَالِمُ الْغَيْبِ وَالشَّهَادَةِ ۖ هُوَ الرَّحْمَٰنُ الرَّحِيمُ ﴿٢٢﴾ هُوَ اللَّهُ الَّذِي لَا إِلَٰهَ إِلَّا هُوَ ۚ الْمَلِكُ الْقُدُّوسُ السَّلَامُ الْمُؤْمِنُ الْمُهَيْمِنُ الْعَزِيزُ الْجَبَّارُ الْمُتَكَبِّرُ ۚ سُبْحَانَ اللَّهِ عَمَّا يُشْرِكُونَ ﴿٢٣﴾ هُوَ اللَّهُ الْخَالِقُ الْبَارِئُ الْمُصَوِّرُ ۖ لَهُ الْأَسْمَاءُ الْحُسْنَىٰ ۚ يُسَبِّحُ لَهُ مَا فِي السَّمَاوَاتِ وَالْأَرْضِ ۖ وَهُوَ الْعَزِيزُ الْحَكِيمُ ﴿٢٤﴾ [الحشر:21-24]

Law anzalna hatha alqurana AAala jabalin laraaytahu
khashiAAan mutasaddiAAan min khashyati Allahi watilka
alamthalu nadribuha lilnnasi laAAallahum yatafakkaroona
(21) Huwa Allahu allathee la ilaha illa huwa AAalimu alghaybi
waalshshahadati huwa alrrahmanu alrraheemu (22) Huwa Allahu
allathee la ilaha illa huwa almaliku alquddoosu alssalamu
almuminu almuhayminu alAAazeezu aljabbaru almutakabbiru
subhana Allahi AAamma yushrikoona (23) Huwa Allahu alkhaliqu
albario almusawwiru lahu alasmao alhusna yusabbihu lahu ma fee
alssamawati waalardi wahuwa alAAazeezu alhakeemu (24)

If We had sent down this Qur'an upon a mountain, you would
have seen it humbled and coming apart from fear of Allah. And
these examples We present to the people that perhaps they will
give thought. (21) He is Allah, other than whom there is no deity,
Knower of the unseen and the witnessed. He is the Entirely
Merciful, the Especially Merciful. (22) He is Allah, other than
whom there is no deity, the Sovereign, the Pure, the Perfection, the
Bestower of Faith, the Overseer, the Exalted in Might, the
Compeller, the Superior. Exalted is Allah above whatever they
associate with Him. (23) He is Allah, the Creator, the Inventor,
the Fashioner; to Him belong the best names. Whatever is in the
heavens and earth is exalting Him. And He is the Exalted in
Might, the Wise. (24)

وَإِن يَكَادُ الَّذِينَ كَفَرُوا لَيُزْلِقُونَكَ بِأَبْصَارِهِمْ لَمَّا سَمِعُوا الذِّكْرَ وَيَقُولُونَ إِنَّهُ لَمَجْنُونٌ

﴿٥١﴾ وَمَا هُوَ إِلَّا ذِكْرٌ لِّلْعَالَمِينَ ﴿٥٢﴾ [القلم: 51-52]

Wain yakadu allatheena kafaroo layuzliqoonaka biabsarihim
lamma samiAAoo alththikra wayaqooloona innahu lamajnoonun
(51) Wama huwa illa thikrun lilAAalameena (52)

And indeed, those who disbelieve would almost make you slip with
their eyes when they hear the message, and they say, "Indeed, he is
mad." (51) But it is not except a reminder to the worlds. (52)

وَأَنَّهُ تَعَالَىٰ جَدُّ رَبِّنَا مَا اتَّخَذَ صَاحِبَةً وَلَا وَلَدًا ﴿٣﴾ [الجن: 03]

Waannahu taAAala jaddu rabbina ma ittakhatha sahibatan wala
waladan (3)

And [it teaches] that exalted is the nobleness of our Lord; He has
not taken a wife or a son (3)

بِسْمِ اللَّهِ الرَّحْمَٰنِ الرَّحِيمِ

Bismi Allahi alrrahmani alrraheem

In the name of Allah, the Entirely Merciful, the Especially Merciful

قُلْ هُوَ اللَّهُ أَحَدٌ ﴿١﴾ اللَّهُ الصَّمَدُ ﴿٢﴾ لَمْ يَلِدْ وَلَمْ يُولَدْ ﴿٣﴾ وَلَمْ يَكُن لَّهُ كُفُوًا أَحَدٌ ﴿٤﴾ [الإخلاص: 1-4]

Qul huwa Allahu ahadun (1) Allahu alssamadu (2) Lam yalid walam yooladu (3) Walam yakun lahu kufuwan ahadun (4)

Say, "He is Allah, [who is] One, (1) Allah, the Eternal Refuge. (2) He neither begets nor is born, (3) Nor is there to Him any equivalent." (4)

بِسْمِ اللَّهِ الرَّحْمَٰنِ الرَّحِيمِ

Bismi Allahi alrrahmani alrraheemi

In the name of Allah, the Entirely Merciful, the Especially Merciful

قُلْ أَعُوذُ بِرَبِّ الْفَلَقِ ﴿١﴾ مِن شَرِّ مَا خَلَقَ ﴿٢﴾ وَمِن شَرِّ غَاسِقٍ إِذَا وَقَبَ ﴿٣﴾ وَمِن شَرِّ النَّفَّاثَاتِ فِي الْعُقَدِ ﴿٤﴾ وَمِن شَرِّ حَاسِدٍ إِذَا حَسَدَ ﴿٥﴾
[الفلق: 1-5]

Qul aAAoothu birabbi alfalaqi (1) Min sharri ma khalaqa
(2) Wamin sharri ghasiqin itha waqaba (3) Wamin sharri
alnnaffathati fee alAAuqadi (4) Wamin sharri hasidin itha hasada
(5)

Say, "I seek refuge in the Lord of daybreak (1) From the evil of
that which He created (2) And from the evil of darkness when it
settles (3) And from the evil of the blowers in knots (4) And from
the evil of an envier when he envies." (5)

121

بِسْمِ اللَّهِ الرَّحْمَٰنِ الرَّحِيمِ

Bismi Allahi alrrahmani alrraheemi

In the name of Allah, the Entirely Merciful, the Especially Merciful

قُلْ أَعُوذُ بِرَبِّ النَّاسِ ﴿١﴾ مَلِكِ النَّاسِ ﴿٢﴾ إِلَٰهِ النَّاسِ ﴿٣﴾ مِن شَرِّ
الْوَسْوَاسِ الْخَنَّاسِ ﴿٤﴾ الَّذِي يُوَسْوِسُ فِي صُدُورِ النَّاسِ ﴿٥﴾ مِنَ الْجِنَّةِ
وَالنَّاسِ ﴿٦﴾ [الناس: 1-5]

Qul aAAoothu birabbi alnnasi (1) Maliki alnnasi (2) Ilahi alnnasi
(3) Min sharri alwaswasi alkhannasi (4) Allathee yuwaswisu fee
sudoori alnnasi (5) Mina aljinnati wa alnnasm (6)

Say, "I seek refuge in the Lord of mankind, (1) The Sovereign of
mankind. (2) The God of mankind, (3) From the evil of the
retreating whisperer - (4) Who whispers [evil] into the breasts of
mankind - (5) From among the Jinn and mankind." (6)

Ruqya Verses for Evil Eye

أعوذ بالله السميع العليم من الشيطان الرجيم

A'udhu Billahi min ash shaytaani'r rajeem

I seek refuge with Allah from Shaytan the accursed

بِسْمِ اللَّهِ الرَّحْمَٰنِ الرَّحِيمِ

Bismi Allahi alrrahmani alrraheemi

In the name of Allah, the Entirely Merciful, the Especially Merciful

❖ بِسْمِ اللَّهِ الرَّحْمَٰنِ الرَّحِيمِ ﴿١﴾ الْحَمْدُ لِلَّهِ رَبِّ الْعَالَمِينَ ﴿٢﴾ الرَّحْمَٰنِ الرَّحِيمِ ﴿٣﴾ مَالِكِ يَوْمِ الدِّينِ ﴿٤﴾ إِيَّاكَ نَعْبُدُ وَإِيَّاكَ نَسْتَعِينُ ﴿٥﴾ اهْدِنَا الصِّرَاطَ الْمُسْتَقِيمَ ﴿٦﴾ صِرَاطَ الَّذِينَ أَنْعَمْتَ عَلَيْهِمْ غَيْرِ الْمَغْضُوبِ عَلَيْهِمْ وَلَا الضَّالِّينَ [الفاتحة: 7-1]

Bismi Allahi alrrahmani alrraheemi (1) Alhamdu lillahi rabbi alAAalameena (2) Alrrahmani alrraheemi (3) Maliki yawmi alddeeni (4) Iyyaka naAAbudu waiyyaka nastaAAeenu (5) Ihdina alssirata almustaqeema (6) Sirata allatheena anAAamta AAalayhim ghayri almaghdoobi AAalayhim wala alddalleena (7)

In the name of Allah, the Entirely Merciful, the Especially Merciful. (1) [All] praise is [due] to Allah, Lord of the worlds - (2) The Entirely Merciful, the Especially Merciful, (3) Sovereign of the Day of Recompense. (4) It is You we worship and You we ask for help. (5) Guide us to the straight path - (6) The path of those upon whom You have bestowed favour, not of those who have evoked [Your] anger or of those who are astray. (7)

124

بِسْمِ اللَّهِ الرَّحْمَٰنِ الرَّحِيمِ

Bismi All<u>a</u>hi arra<u>h</u>m<u>a</u>ni alrra<u>h</u>eemi

In the name of Allah, the Entirely Merciful, the Especially Merciful

الم ﴿١﴾ ذَٰلِكَ الْكِتَابُ لَا رَيْبَ ۛ فِيهِ ۛ هُدًى لِّلْمُتَّقِينَ ﴿٢﴾ الَّذِينَ يُؤْمِنُونَ بِالْغَيْبِ وَيُقِيمُونَ الصَّلَاةَ وَمِمَّا رَزَقْنَاهُمْ يُنفِقُونَ ﴿٣﴾ وَالَّذِينَ يُؤْمِنُونَ بِمَا أُنزِلَ إِلَيْكَ وَمَا أُنزِلَ مِن قَبْلِكَ وَبِالْآخِرَةِ هُمْ يُوقِنُونَ ﴿٤﴾ أُولَٰئِكَ عَلَىٰ هُدًى مِّن رَّبِّهِمْ ۖ وَأُولَٰئِكَ هُمُ الْمُفْلِحُونَ ﴿٥﴾ [البقرة: 1-5]

Aliflammeem (1) Thalika alkitabu la rayba feehi hudan lilmuttaqeena (2) Allatheena yuminoona bialghaybi wayuqeemoona alssalata wamimma razaqnahum yunfiqoona (3) Waallatheena yuminoona bima onzila ilayka wama onzila min qablika wabialakhirati hum yooqinoona (4) Olaika AAala hudan min rabbihim waolaika humu almuflihoona (5)

Alif, Lam, Meem. (1) This is the Book about which there is no doubt, a guidance for those conscious of Allah - (2) Who believe in the unseen, establish prayer, and spend out of what We have provided for them, (3) And who believe in what has been revealed to you, [O Muhammad], and what was revealed before you, and of the Hereafter they are certain [in faith]. (4) Those are upon [right] guidance from their Lord, and it is those who are the successful. (5)

125

يَكَادُ الْبَرْقُ يَخْطَفُ أَبْصَارَهُمْ ۖ كُلَّمَا أَضَاءَ لَهُم مَّشَوْا فِيهِ وَإِذَا أَظْلَمَ عَلَيْهِمْ قَامُوا ۚ وَلَوْ
شَاءَ اللَّهُ لَذَهَبَ بِسَمْعِهِمْ وَأَبْصَارِهِمْ ۚ إِنَّ اللَّهَ عَلَىٰ كُلِّ شَيْءٍ قَدِيرٌ ﴿٢٠﴾
[البقرة : 20]

Yakadu albarqu yakhtafu absarahum kullama adaa lahum mashaw
feehi waitha athlama AAalayhim qamoo walaw shaa Allahu
lathahaba bisamAAihim waabsarihim inna Allaha AAala kulli
shayin qadeerun (20)

The lightning almost snatches away their sight. Every time it lights
[the way] for them, they walk therein; but when darkness comes
over them, they stand [still]. And if Allah had willed, He could
have taken away their hearing and their sight. Indeed, Allah is over
all things competent. (20)

۞ وَإِذِ اسْتَسْقَىٰ مُوسَىٰ لِقَوْمِهِ فَقُلْنَا اضْرِب بِّعَصَاكَ الْحَجَرَ ۖ فَانفَجَرَتْ مِنْهُ اثْنَتَا
عَشْرَةَ عَيْنًا ۖ قَدْ عَلِمَ كُلُّ أُنَاسٍ مَّشْرَبَهُمْ ۖ كُلُوا وَاشْرَبُوا مِن رِّزْقِ اللَّهِ وَلَا تَعْثَوْا فِي
الْأَرْضِ مُفْسِدِينَ ﴿٦٠﴾ [البقرة : 60]

Waithi istasqa moosa liqawmihi faqulna idrib biAAasaka alhajara
fainfajarat minhu ithnata AAashrata AAaynan qad AAalima kullu
onasin mashrabahum kuloo waishraboo min rizqi Allahi wala
(taAAthaw fee alardi mufsideena (60

And [recall] when Moses prayed for water for his people, so We
said, "Strike with your staff the stone." And there gushed forth
from it twelve springs, and every people knew its watering place.
"Eat and drink from the provision of Allah, and do not commit
(abuse on the earth, spreading corruption." (60

قَالُوا ادْعُ لَنَا رَبَّكَ يُبَيِّن لَّنَا مَا لَوْنُهَا ۚ قَالَ إِنَّهُ يَقُولُ إِنَّهَا بَقَرَةٌ صَفْرَاءُ فَاقِعٌ لَّوْنُهَا تَسُرُّ النَّاظِرِينَ ﴿٦٩﴾ [البقرة: 69]

Qaloo odAAu lana rabbaka yubayyin lana ma lawnuha qala innahu yaqoolu innaha baqaratun safrao faqiAAun lawnuha tasurru alnnathireena (69)

They said, "Call upon your Lord to show us what is her color." He said, "He says, 'It is a yellow cow, bright in color - pleasing to the observers.' (69)

وَدَّ كَثِيرٌ مِّنْ أَهْلِ الْكِتَابِ لَوْ يَرُدُّونَكُم مِّن بَعْدِ إِيمَانِكُمْ كُفَّارًا حَسَدًا مِّنْ عِندِ أَنفُسِهِم مِّن بَعْدِ مَا تَبَيَّنَ لَهُمُ الْحَقُّ ۖ فَاعْفُوا وَاصْفَحُوا حَتَّىٰ يَأْتِيَ اللَّهُ بِأَمْرِهِ ۗ إِنَّ اللَّهَ عَلَىٰ كُلِّ شَيْءٍ قَدِيرٌ ﴿١٠٩﴾ [البقرة: 109]

Wadda katheerun min ahli alkitabi law yaruddoonakum min baAAdi eemanikum kuffaran hasadan min AAindi anfusihim min baAAdi ma tabayyana lahumu alhaqqu faoAAfoo waisfahoo hatta yatiya Allahu biamrihi inna Allaha AAala kulli shayin qadeerun (109)

Many of the People of the Scripture wish they could turn you back to disbelief after you have believed, out of envy from themselves [even] after the truth has become clear to them. So pardon and overlook until Allah delivers His command. Indeed, Allah is over all things competent. (109)

اللَّهُ لَا إِلَٰهَ إِلَّا هُوَ الْحَيُّ الْقَيُّومُ ۚ لَا تَأْخُذُهُ سِنَةٌ وَلَا نَوْمٌ ۚ لَهُ مَا فِي السَّمَاوَاتِ وَمَا فِي الْأَرْضِ ۗ مَن ذَا الَّذِي يَشْفَعُ عِندَهُ إِلَّا بِإِذْنِهِ ۚ يَعْلَمُ مَا بَيْنَ أَيْدِيهِمْ وَمَا خَلْفَهُمْ ۖ وَلَا يُحِيطُونَ بِشَيْءٍ مِّنْ عِلْمِهِ إِلَّا بِمَا شَاءَ ۚ وَسِعَ كُرْسِيُّهُ السَّمَاوَاتِ وَالْأَرْضَ ۖ وَلَا يَئُودُهُ حِفْظُهُمَا ۚ وَهُوَ الْعَلِيُّ الْعَظِيمُ ﴿٢٥٥﴾ [البقرة: 255]

Allahu la ilaha illa huwa alhayyu alqayyoomu la takhuthuhu sinatun wala nawmun lahu ma fee alssamawati wama fee alardi man tha allathee yashfaAAu AAindahu illa biithnihi yaAAlamu ma bayna aydeehim wama khalfahum wala yuheetoona bishayin min AAilmihi illa bima shaa wasiAAa kursiyyuhu alssamawati waalarda wala yaooduhu hifthuhuma wahuwa alAAaliyyu alAAatheemu (255)

Allah - there is no deity except Him, the Ever-Living, the Sustainer of [all] existence. Neither drowsiness overtakes Him nor sleep. To Him belongs whatever is in the heavens and whatever is on the earth. Who is it that can intercede with Him except by His permission? He knows what is [presently] before them and what will be after them, and they encompass not a thing of His knowledge except for what He wills. His Kursi extends over the heavens and the earth, and their preservation tires Him not. And He is the Most High, the Most Great. (255)

128

آمَنَ الرَّسُولُ بِمَا أُنزِلَ إِلَيْهِ مِن رَّبِّهِ وَالْمُؤْمِنُونَ ۚ كُلٌّ آمَنَ بِاللَّهِ وَمَلَائِكَتِهِ وَكُتُبِهِ وَرُسُلِهِ لَا نُفَرِّقُ بَيْنَ أَحَدٍ مِّن رُّسُلِهِ ۚ وَقَالُوا سَمِعْنَا وَأَطَعْنَا ۖ غُفْرَانَكَ رَبَّنَا وَإِلَيْكَ الْمَصِيرُ ﴿٢٨٥﴾ لَا يُكَلِّفُ اللَّهُ نَفْسًا إِلَّا وُسْعَهَا ۚ لَهَا مَا كَسَبَتْ وَعَلَيْهَا مَا اكْتَسَبَتْ ۗ رَبَّنَا لَا تُؤَاخِذْنَا إِن نَّسِينَا أَوْ أَخْطَأْنَا ۚ رَبَّنَا وَلَا تَحْمِلْ عَلَيْنَا إِصْرًا كَمَا حَمَلْتَهُ عَلَى الَّذِينَ مِن قَبْلِنَا ۚ رَبَّنَا وَلَا تُحَمِّلْنَا مَا لَا طَاقَةَ لَنَا بِهِ ۖ وَاعْفُ عَنَّا وَاغْفِرْ لَنَا وَارْحَمْنَا ۚ أَنتَ مَوْلَانَا فَانصُرْنَا عَلَى الْقَوْمِ الْكَافِرِينَ ﴿٢٨٦﴾

[البقرة: 285-286]

Amana alrrasoolu bima onzila ilayhi min rabbihi waalmuminoona kullun amana biAllahi wamalaikatihi wakutubihi warusulihi la nufarriqu bayna ahadin min rusulihi waqaloo samiAAna waataAAna ghufranaka rabbana wailayka almaseeru (285) La yukallifu Allahu nafsan illa wusAAaha laha ma kasabat waAAalayha ma iktasabat rabbana la tuakhithna in naseena aw akhtana rabbana wala tahmil AAalayna isran kama hamaltahu AAala allatheena min qablina rabbana wala tuhammilna ma la taqata lana bihi waoAAfu AAanna waighfir lana wairhamna anta mawlana faonsurna AAala alqawmi alkafireena (286)

The Messenger has believed in what was revealed to him from his Lord, and [so have] the believers. All of them have believed in Allah and His angels and His books and His messengers, [saying], "We make no distinction between any of His messengers." And they say, "We hear and we obey. [We seek] Your forgiveness, our Lord, and to You is the [final] destination." (285) Allah does not charge a soul except [with that within] its capacity. It will have [the consequence of] what [good] it has gained, and it will bear [the consequence of] what [evil] it has earned. "Our Lord, do not impose blame upon us if we have forgotten or erred. Our Lord, and lay not upon us a burden like that which You laid upon those before us. Our Lord, and burden us not with that which we have no ability to bear. And pardon us; and forgive us; and have mercy upon us. You are our protector, so give us victory over the disbelieving people." (286)

وَلَا تَتَمَنَّوْا مَا فَضَّلَ اللَّهُ بِهِ بَعْضَكُمْ عَلَىٰ بَعْضٍ ۚ لِّلرِّجَالِ نَصِيبٌ مِّمَّا اكْتَسَبُوا ۖ وَلِلنِّسَاءِ نَصِيبٌ مِّمَّا اكْتَسَبْنَ ۚ وَاسْأَلُوا اللَّهَ مِن فَضْلِهِ ۗ إِنَّ اللَّهَ كَانَ بِكُلِّ شَيْءٍ عَلِيمًا

﴿٣٢﴾ [النساء: 32]

Wala tatamannaw ma faddala Allahu bihi baAAdakum AAala baAAdin lilrrijali naseebun mimma iktasaboo walilnnisai naseebun mimma iktasabna waisaloo Allaha min fadlihi inna Allaha kana bikulli shayin AAaleeman (32)

And do not wish for that by which Allah has made some of you exceed others. For men is a share of what they have earned, and for women is a share of what they have earned. And ask Allah of his bounty. Indeed Allah is ever, of all things, Knowing. (32)

أَمْ يَحْسُدُونَ النَّاسَ عَلَىٰ مَا آتَاهُمُ اللَّهُ مِن فَضْلِهِ ۖ فَقَدْ آتَيْنَا آلَ إِبْرَاهِيمَ الْكِتَابَ وَالْحِكْمَةَ وَآتَيْنَاهُم مُّلْكًا عَظِيمًا ﴿٥٤﴾ [النساء: 54]

Am yahsudoona alnnasa AAala ma atahumu Allahu min fadlihi faqad atayna ala ibraheema alkitaba waalhikmata waataynahum mulkan AAatheeman (54)

Or do they envy people for what Allah has given them of His bounty? But we had already given the family of Abraham the Scripture and wisdom and conferred upon them a great kingdom. (54)

لَّا تُدْرِكُهُ الْأَبْصَارُ وَهُوَ يُدْرِكُ الْأَبْصَارَ ۖ وَهُوَ اللَّطِيفُ الْخَبِيرُ ﴿١٠٣﴾ [الأنعام: 103]

La tudrikuhu alabsaru wahuwa yudriku alabsara wahuwa allateefu alkhabeeru (103)

Vision perceives Him not, but He perceives [all] vision; and He is the Subtle, the Acquainted. (103)

$$فَلَا تُعْجِبْكَ أَمْوَالُهُمْ وَلَا أَوْلَادُهُمْ ۚ إِنَّمَا يُرِيدُ اللَّهُ لِيُعَذِّبَهُمْ بِهَا فِي الْحَيَاةِ الدُّنْيَا وَتَزْهَقَ أَنفُسُهُمْ وَهُمْ كَافِرُونَ ﴿٥٥﴾ [التوبة: 55]$$

So let not their wealth or their children impress you. Allah only intends to punish them through them in worldly life and that their (55) .souls should depart [at death] while they are disbelievers

Fala tuAAjibka amwaluhum wala awladuhum innama yureedu Allahu liyuAAaththibahum biha fee alhayati alddunya watazhaqa anfusuhum wahum kafiroona (55)

$$وَقَالَ يَا بَنِيَّ لَا تَدْخُلُوا مِن بَابٍ وَاحِدٍ وَادْخُلُوا مِنْ أَبْوَابٍ مُّتَفَرِّقَةٍ ۖ وَمَا أُغْنِي عَنكُم مِّنَ اللَّهِ مِن شَيْءٍ ۖ إِنِ الْحُكْمُ إِلَّا لِلَّهِ ۖ عَلَيْهِ تَوَكَّلْتُ ۖ وَعَلَيْهِ فَلْيَتَوَكَّلِ الْمُتَوَكِّلُونَ ﴿٦٧﴾ [يوسف:67]$$

Waqala ya baniyya la tadkhuloo min babin wahidin waodkhuloo min abwabin mutafarriqatin wama oghnee AAankum mina Allahi min shayin ini alhukmu illa lillahi AAalayhi tawakkaltu waAAalayhi falyatawakkali almutawakkiloona (67)

And he said, "O my sons, do not enter from one gate but enter from different gates; and I cannot avail you against [the decree of] Allah at all. The decision is only for Allah; upon Him I have relied, and upon Him let those who would rely [indeed] rely." (67)

$$وَوَحْيِنَا وَلَا تُخَاطِبْنِي فِي الَّذِينَ ظَلَمُوا إِنَّهُم مُّغْرَقُونَ بِأَعْيُنِنَا وَاصْنَعِ الْفُلْكَ$$

$$[هود : 37]$$

WaisnaAAi alfulka biaAAyunina wawahyina wala tukhatibnee fee allatheena thalamoo innahum mughraqoona (37)

And construct the ship under Our observation and Our inspiration and do not address Me concerning those who have wronged; indeed, they are [to be] drowned." (37)

وَلَقَدْ جَعَلْنَا فِي السَّمَاءِ بُرُوجًا وَزَيَّنَّاهَا لِلنَّاظِرِينَ ﴿١٦﴾ وَحَفِظْنَاهَا مِن كُلِّ شَيْطَانٍ رَّجِيمٍ ﴿١٧﴾ إِلَّا مَنِ اسْتَرَقَ السَّمْعَ فَأَتْبَعَهُ شِهَابٌ مُّبِينٌ ﴿١٨﴾ [الحجر: 16-18]

Walaqad jaAAalna fee alssamai buroojan wazayyannaha lilnnathireena (16) Wahafithnaha min kulli shaytanin rajeemin (17) Illa mani istaraqa alssamAAa faatbaAAahu shihabun mubeenun (18)

And We have placed within the heaven great stars and have beautified it for the observers. (16) And We have protected it from every devil expelled [from the mercy of Allah] (17) Except one who steals a hearing and is pursued by a clear burning flame. (18)

وَلَا تَمُدَّنَّ عَيْنَيْكَ إِلَىٰ مَا مَتَّعْنَا بِهِ أَزْوَاجًا مِّنْهُمْ زَهْرَةَ الْحَيَاةِ الدُّنْيَا لِنَفْتِنَهُمْ فِيهِ وَرِزْقُ رَبِّكَ خَيْرٌ وَأَبْقَىٰ ﴿١٣١﴾ [طه:131]

And do not extend your eyes toward that by which We have given enjoyment to [some] categories of them, [its being but] the splendor of worldly life by which We test them. And the provision of your Lord is better and more enduring. (131)

Wala tamuddanna AAaynayka ila ma mattaAAna bihi azwajan minhum zahrata alhayati alddunya linaftinahum feehi warizqu rabbika khayrun waabqa (131)

فَخَرَجَ عَلَىٰ قَوْمِهِ فِي زِينَتِهِ قَالَ الَّذِينَ يُرِيدُونَ الْحَيَاةَ الدُّنْيَا يَا لَيْتَ لَنَا مِثْلَ مَا أُوتِيَ قَارُونُ إِنَّهُ لَذُو حَظٍّ عَظِيمٍ ﴿٧٩﴾ [القصص : 79]

Fakharaja AAala qawmihi fee zeenatihi qala allatheena yureedoona alhayata alddunya ya layta lana mithla ma ootiya qaroonu innahu lathoo haththin AAatheemin (79)

So he came out before his people in his adornment. Those who desired the worldly life said, "Oh, would that we had like what was given to Qarun. Indeed, he is one of great fortune." (79)

وَلَوْلَا إِذْ دَخَلْتَ جَنَّتَكَ قُلْتَ مَا شَاءَ اللَّهُ لَا قُوَّةَ إِلَّا بِاللَّهِ ۚ إِن تَرَنِ أَنَا أَقَلَّ مِنكَ مَالًا وَوَلَدًا ﴿٣٩﴾ [الكهف:39]

Walawla ith dakhalta jannataka qulta ma shaa Allahu la quwwata illa biAllahi in tarani ana aqalla minka malan wawaladan (39)

And why did you, when you entered your garden, not say, 'What Allah willed [has occurred]; there is no power except in Allah'? Although you see me less than you in wealth and children, (39)

فَنَظَرَ نَظْرَةً فِي النُّجُومِ ﴿٨٨﴾ فَقَالَ إِنِّي سَقِيمٌ ﴿٨٩﴾ فَتَوَلَّوْا عَنْهُ مُدْبِرِينَ ﴿٩٠﴾ [الصافات: 88 - 90]

Fanathara nathratan fee alnnujoomi (88) Faqala innee saqeemun (89) Fatawallaw AAanhu mudbireena (90)

And he cast a look at the stars (88) And said, "Indeed, I am [about to be] ill." (89) So they turned away from him, departing. (90)

سَيَقُولُ الْمُخَلَّفُونَ إِذَا انطَلَقْتُمْ إِلَىٰ مَغَانِمَ لِتَأْخُذُوهَا ذَرُونَا نَتَّبِعْكُمْ ۖ يُرِيدُونَ أَن يُبَدِّلُوا كَلَامَ اللَّهِ ۚ قُل لَّن تَتَّبِعُونَا كَذَٰلِكُمْ قَالَ اللَّهُ مِن قَبْلُ ۚ فَسَيَقُولُونَ بَلْ تَحْسُدُونَنَا ۚ بَلْ كَانُوا لَا يَفْقَهُونَ إِلَّا قَلِيلًا ﴿١٥﴾ [الفتح : 15]

Sayaqoolu almukhallafoona itha intalaqtum ila maghanima litakhuthooha tharoona nattabiAAkum yureedoona an yubaddiloo kalama Allahi qul lan tattabiAAoona kathalikum qala Allahu min qablu fasayaqooloona bal tahsudoonana bal kanoo la yafqahoona illa qaleelan (15)

Those who remained behind will say when you set out toward the war booty to take it, "Let us follow you." They wish to change the words of Allah. Say, "Never will you follow us. Thus did Allah say before." So they will say, "Rather, you envy us." But [in fact] they were not understanding except a little. (15)

134

بِسْمِ اللهِ الرَّحْمَنِ الرَّحِيمِ

﴿ تَبَارَكَ الَّذِي بِيَدِهِ الْمُلْكُ وَهُوَ عَلَىٰ كُلِّ شَيْءٍ قَدِيرٌ ﴿١﴾ الَّذِي خَلَقَ الْمَوْتَ
وَالْحَيَاةَ لِيَبْلُوَكُمْ أَيُّكُمْ أَحْسَنُ عَمَلًا ۚ وَهُوَ الْعَزِيزُ الْغَفُورُ ﴿٢﴾ الَّذِي خَلَقَ سَبْعَ
سَمَاوَاتٍ طِبَاقًا ۖ مَا تَرَىٰ فِي خَلْقِ الرَّحْمَٰنِ مِن تَفَاوُتٍ ۖ فَارْجِعِ الْبَصَرَ هَلْ تَرَىٰ مِن
فُطُورٍ ﴿٣﴾ ثُمَّ ارْجِعِ الْبَصَرَ كَرَّتَيْنِ يَنقَلِبْ إِلَيْكَ الْبَصَرُ خَاسِئًا وَهُوَ حَسِيرٌ
﴿٤﴾ [الملك: 1-4]

Tabaraka allathee biyadihi almulku wahuwa AAala kulli shayin
qadeerun (1) Allathee khalaqa almawta waalhayata liyabluwakum
ayyukum ahsanu AAamalan wahuwa alAAazeezu alghafooru
(2) Allathee khalaqa sabAAa samawatin tibaqan ma tara fee khalqi
alrrahmani min tafawutin fairjiAAi albasara hal tara min futoorin
(3) Thumma irjiAAi albasara karratayni yanqalib ilayka albasaru
khasian wahuwa haseerun (4)

Blessed is He in whose hand is dominion, and He is over all things
competent - (1) [He] who created death and life to test you [as to]
which of you is best in deed - and He is the Exalted in Might, the
Forgiving - (2) [And] who created seven heavens in layers. You do
not see in the creation of the Most Merciful any inconsistency. So
return [your] vision [to the sky]; do you see any breaks? (3) Then
return [your] vision twice again. [Your] vision will return to you
humbled while it is fatigued. (4)

بِسْمِ اللَّهِ الرَّحْمَٰنِ الرَّحِيمِ

۞ ن ۚ وَالْقَلَمِ وَمَا يَسْطُرُونَ ﴿١﴾ مَا أَنتَ بِنِعْمَةِ رَبِّكَ بِمَجْنُونٍ ﴿٢﴾ وَإِنَّ لَكَ لَأَجْرًا غَيْرَ مَمْنُونٍ ﴿٣﴾ وَإِنَّكَ لَعَلَىٰ خُلُقٍ عَظِيمٍ ﴿٤﴾ فَسَتُبْصِرُ وَيُبْصِرُونَ ﴿٥﴾ [القلم:1-5]

Noon waalqalami wama yasṭuroona (1) Ma anta biniAAmati rabbika bimajnoonin (2) Wainna laka laajran ghayra mamnoonin (3) Wainnaka laAAala khuluqin AAa_th_eemin (4) Fasatubṣiru wayubṣiroona (5)

Nun. By the pen and what they inscribe, (1) You are not, [O Muhammad], by the favor of your Lord, a madman. (2) And indeed, for you is a reward uninterrupted. (3) And indeed, you are of a great moral character. (4) So you will see and they will see (5)

وَإِن يَكَادُ الَّذِينَ كَفَرُوا لَيُزْلِقُونَكَ بِأَبْصَارِهِمْ لَمَّا سَمِعُوا الذِّكْرَ وَيَقُولُونَ إِنَّهُ لَمَجْنُونٌ ﴿٥١﴾ [القلم:51]

Wain yaka_d_u alla_th_eena kafaroo layuzliqoonaka biabṣarihim lamma samiAAoo al_thth_ikra wayaqooloona innahu lamajnoonun (51)

And indeed, those who disbelieve would almost make you slip with their eyes when they hear the message, and they say, "Indeed, he is mad." (51)

وَاصْبِرْ لِحُكْمِ رَبِّكَ فَإِنَّكَ بِأَعْيُنِنَا وَسَبِّحْ بِحَمْدِ رَبِّكَ حِينَ تَقُومُ ﴿٤٨﴾

[الطور : 48]

Waisbir lihukmi rabbika fainnaka biaAAyunina wasabbih bihamdi
rabbika heena taqoomu (48)

And be patient, [O Muhammad], for the decision of your Lord, for
indeed, you are in Our eyes. And exalt [Allah] with praise of your
Lord when you arise. (48)

❖ وَإِذَا رَأَيْتَهُمْ تُعْجِبُكَ أَجْسَامُهُمْ وَإِن يَقُولُوا تَسْمَعْ لِقَوْلِهِمْ كَأَنَّهُمْ خُشُبٌ
مُسَنَّدَةٌ يَحْسَبُونَ كُلَّ صَيْحَةٍ عَلَيْهِمْ هُمُ الْعَدُوُّ فَاحْذَرْهُمْ قَاتَلَهُمُ اللَّهُ أَنَّى
يُؤْفَكُونَ ﴿٤﴾ [المنافقون: 4]

Waitha raaytahum tuAAjibuka ajsamuhum wain yaqooloo
tasmaAA liqawlihim kaannahum khushubun musannadatun
yahsaboona kulla sayhatin AAalayhim humu alAAaduwwu
faihtharhum qatalahumu Allahu anna yufakoona (4)

And when you see them, their forms please you, and if they speak,
you listen to their speech. [They are] as if they were pieces of wood
propped up - they think that every shout is against them. They are
the enemy, so beware of them. May Allah destroy them; how are
they deluded? (4)

عَيْنًا يَشْرَبُ بِهَا عِبَادُ اللَّهِ يُفَجِّرُونَهَا تَفْجِيرًا ﴿٦﴾ [الإنسان : 6]

AAaynan yashrabu biha AAibadu Allahi yufajjiroonaha tafjeeran
(6)

A spring of which the [righteous] servants of Allah will drink; they
will make it gush forth in force [and abundance]. (6)

137

قَاتِلُوهُمْ يُعَذِّبْهُمُ اللَّهُ بِأَيْدِيكُمْ وَيُخْزِهِمْ وَيَنصُرْكُمْ عَلَيْهِمْ وَيَشْفِ صُدُورَ قَوْمٍ مُّؤْمِنِينَ وَاللَّهُ عَلِيمٌ ۝ وَيَتُوبُ اللَّهُ عَلَىٰ مَن يَشَاءُ ۗ وَيُذْهِبْ غَيْظَ قُلُوبِهِمْ ﴿١٤﴾ حَكِيمٌ ﴿١٥﴾ [التوبة:14-15]

Qatiloohum yuAAaththibhumu Allahu biaydeekum wayukhzihim wayansurkum AAalayhim wayashfi sudoora qawmin mumineena (14) Wayuthhib ghaytha quloobihim wayatoobu Allahu AAala man yashao waAllahu AAaleemun hakeemun (15)

Fight them; Allah will punish them by your hands and will disgrace them and give you victory over them and satisfy the breasts of a believing people (14) And remove the fury in the believers' hearts. And Allah turns in forgiveness to whom He wills; and Allah is Knowing and Wise. (15)

يَا أَيُّهَا النَّاسُ قَدْ جَاءَتْكُم مَّوْعِظَةٌ مِّن رَّبِّكُمْ وَشِفَاءٌ لِّمَا فِي الصُّدُورِ وَهُدًى وَرَحْمَةٌ لِّلْمُؤْمِنِينَ ﴿٥٧﴾ [يونس: 57]

Ya ayyuha alnnasu qad jaatkum mawAAithatun min rabbikum washifaon lima fee alssudoori wahudan warahmatun lilmumineena (57)

O mankind, there has to come to you instruction from your Lord and healing for what is in the breasts and guidance and mercy for the believers. (57)

وَأَوْحَىٰ رَبُّكَ إِلَى النَّحْلِ أَنِ اتَّخِذِي مِنَ الْجِبَالِ بُيُوتًا وَمِنَ الشَّجَرِ وَمِمَّا يَعْرِشُونَ ﴿٦٨﴾ ثُمَّ كُلِي مِن كُلِّ الثَّمَرَاتِ فَاسْلُكِي سُبُلَ رَبِّكِ ذُلُلًا ۚ يَخْرُجُ مِن بُطُونِهَا شَرَابٌ مُّخْتَلِفٌ أَلْوَانُهُ فِيهِ شِفَاءٌ لِّلنَّاسِ ۗ إِنَّ فِي ذَٰلِكَ لَآيَةً لِّقَوْمٍ يَتَفَكَّرُونَ ﴿٦٩﴾ [النحل: 68-69]

Waawha rabbuka ila alnnahli ani ittakhithee mina aljibali buyootan wamina alshshajari wamimma yaAArishoona (68) Thumma kulee min kulli alththamarati faoslukee subula rabbiki thululan yakhruju min butooniha sharabun mukhtalifun alwanuhu feehi shifaon lilnnasi inna fee thalika laayatan liqawmin yatafakkaroona (69)

And your Lord inspired to the bee, "Take for yourself among the mountains, houses, and among the trees and [in] that which they construct. (68)

وَنُنَزِّلُ مِنَ الْقُرْآنِ مَا هُوَ شِفَاءٌ وَرَحْمَةٌ لِّلْمُؤْمِنِينَ ۙ وَلَا يَزِيدُ الظَّالِمِينَ إِلَّا خَسَارًا ﴿٨٢﴾ [الإسراء: 82]

Wanunazzilu mina alqurani ma huwa shifaon warahmatun lilmumineena wala yazeedu alththalimeena illa khasaran (82)

And We send down of the Qur'an that which is healing and mercy for the believers, but it does not increase the wrongdoers except in loss. (82)

وَإِذَا مَرِضْتُ فَهُوَ يَشْفِينِ ﴿٨٠﴾ [الشعراء: 80]

Waitha maridtu fahuwa yashfeeni (80)

And when I am ill, it is He who cures me (80)

139

وَلَوْ جَعَلْنَاهُ قُرْآنًا أَعْجَمِيًّا لَّقَالُوا لَوْلَا فُصِّلَتْ آيَاتُهُ ۖ أَأَعْجَمِيٌّ وَعَرَبِيٌّ ۗ قُلْ هُوَ لِلَّذِينَ
آمَنُوا هُدًى وَشِفَاءٌ ۖ وَالَّذِينَ لَا يُؤْمِنُونَ فِي آذَانِهِمْ وَقْرٌ وَهُوَ عَلَيْهِمْ عَمًى ۚ أُولَٰئِكَ
يُنَادَوْنَ مِن مَّكَانٍ بَعِيدٍ ﴿٤٤﴾ [فصلت: 44]

Walaw jaAAalnahu quranan aAAjamiyyan laqaloo lawla fussilat
ayatuhu aaAAjamiyyun waAAarabiyyun qul huwa lillatheena
amanoo hudan washifaon waallatheena la yuminoona fee
athanihim waqrun wahuwa AAalayhim AAaman olaika
yunadawna min makanin baAAeedin (44)

And if We had made it a non-Arabic Qur'an, they would have
said, "Why are its verses not explained in detail [in our language]?
Is it a foreign [recitation] and an Arab [messenger]?" Say, "It is, for
those who believe, a guidance and cure." And those who do not
believe - in their ears is deafness, and it is upon them blindness.
Those are being called from a distant place. (44)

بِسْمِ اللَّهِ الرَّحْمَٰنِ الرَّحِيمِ

Bismi Allahi alrrahmani alrraheem

In the name of Allah , the Entirely Merciful, the Especially
Merciful

قُلْ هُوَ اللَّهُ أَحَدٌ ﴿١﴾ اللَّهُ الصَّمَدُ ﴿٢﴾ لَمْ يَلِدْ وَلَمْ يُولَدْ ﴿٣﴾ وَلَمْ يَكُن لَّهُ
كُفُوًا أَحَدٌ ﴿٤﴾ [الإخلاص: 1-4]

Qul huwa Allahu ahadun (1) Allahu alssamadu (2) Lam yalid
walam yooladu (3) Walam yakun lahu kufuwan ahadun (4)

Say, "He is Allah, [who is] One, (1) Allah, the Eternal Refuge.
(2) He neither begets nor is born, (3) Nor is there to Him any
equivalent." (4)

بِسْمِ اللَّهِ الرَّحْمَٰنِ الرَّحِيمِ

Bismi Allahi alrrahmani alrraheemi

In the name of Allah, the Entirely Merciful, the Especially Merciful

قُلْ أَعُوذُ بِرَبِّ الْفَلَقِ ﴿١﴾ مِن شَرِّ مَا خَلَقَ ﴿٢﴾ وَمِن شَرِّ غَاسِقٍ إِذَا وَقَبَ ﴿٣﴾ وَمِن شَرِّ النَّفَّاثَاتِ فِي الْعُقَدِ ﴿٤﴾ وَمِن شَرِّ حَاسِدٍ إِذَا حَسَدَ ﴿٥﴾

[الفلق:1-5]

Qul aAAoothu birabbi alfalaqi (1) Min sharri ma khalaqa
(2) Wamin sharri ghasiqin itha waqaba (3) Wamin sharri
alnnaffathati fee alAAuqadi (4) Wamin sharri hasidin itha hasada
(5)

Say, "I seek refuge in the Lord of daybreak (1) From the evil of
that which He created (2) And from the evil of darkness when it
settles (3) And from the evil of the blowers in knots (4) And from
the evil of an envier when he envies." (5)

بِسْمِ اللَّهِ الرَّحْمَٰنِ الرَّحِيمِ

Bismi All*a*hi alrra*h*m*a*ni alrra*h*eemi

In the name of Allah, the Entirely Merciful, the Especially Merciful

قُلْ أَعُوذُ بِرَبِّ النَّاسِ ﴿١﴾ مَلِكِ النَّاسِ ﴿٢﴾ إِلَٰهِ النَّاسِ ﴿٣﴾ مِن شَرِّ الْوَسْوَاسِ الْخَنَّاسِ ﴿٤﴾ الَّذِي يُوَسْوِسُ فِي صُدُورِ النَّاسِ ﴿٥﴾ مِنَ الْجِنَّةِ وَالنَّاسِ ﴿٦﴾ [الناس: 1-5]

Qul aAAoo*thu* birabbi alnn*a*si (1) M*a*liki alnn*a*si (2) Il*a*hi alnn*a*si (3) Min sharri alwasw*a*si alkhann*a*si (4) Alla*thee* yuwaswisu fee *s*udoori alnn*a*si (5) Mina aljinnati wa alnn*a*si (6)

Say, "I seek refuge in the Lord of mankind, (1) The Sovereign of mankind. (2) The God of mankind, (3) From the evil of the retreating whisperer - (4) Who whispers [evil] into the breasts of mankind - (5) From among the Jinn and mankind." (6)

Ruqya Verses for Black Magic

أعوذ بالله السميع العليم من الشيطان الرجيم

A'udhu Billahi min ash shaytaani'r rajeem

I seek refuge with Allah from Shaytan the accursed

بِسْمِ اللَّهِ الرَّحْمَٰنِ الرَّحِيمِ

Bismi Allahi alrrahmani alrraheemi

In the name of Allah, the Entirely Merciful, the Especially Merciful

❀ بِسْمِ اللَّهِ الرَّحْمَٰنِ الرَّحِيمِ ﴿١﴾ الْحَمْدُ لِلَّهِ رَبِّ الْعَالَمِينَ ﴿٢﴾ الرَّحْمَٰنِ
الرَّحِيمِ ﴿٣﴾ مَالِكِ يَوْمِ الدِّينِ ﴿٤﴾ إِيَّاكَ نَعْبُدُ وَإِيَّاكَ نَسْتَعِينُ ﴿٥﴾ اهْدِنَا
الصِّرَاطَ الْمُسْتَقِيمَ ﴿٦﴾ صِرَاطَ الَّذِينَ أَنْعَمْتَ عَلَيْهِمْ غَيْرِ الْمَغْضُوبِ عَلَيْهِمْ وَلَا
الضَّالِّينَ   [الفاتحة: 7:1-]

Bismi Allahi alrrahmani alrraheemi (1) Alhamdu lillahi rabbi
alAAalameena (2) Alrrahmani alrraheemi (3) Maliki yawmi
alddeeni (4) Iyyaka naAAbudu waiyyaka nastaAAeenu (5) Ihdina
alssirata almustaqeema (6) Sirata allatheena anAAamta AAalayhim
ghayri almaghdoobi AAalayhim wala alddalleena (7)

In the name of Allah, the Entirely Merciful, the Especially
Merciful. (1) [All] praise is [due] to Allah, Lord of the worlds - (2)
The Entirely Merciful, the Especially Merciful, (3) Sovereign of the
Day of Recompense. (4) It is You we worship and You we ask for
help. (5) Guide us to the straight path - (6) The path of those upon
whom You have bestowed favour, not of those who have evoked
[Your] anger or of those who are astray. (7)

بِسْمِ اللَّهِ الرَّحْمَٰنِ الرَّحِيمِ

Bismi All_a_hi alrra_h_m_a_ni alrra_h_eemi

In the name of Allah, the Entirely Merciful, the Especially Merciful

الم ﴿١﴾ ذَٰلِكَ الْكِتَابُ لَا رَيْبَ ۛ فِيهِ ۛ هُدًى لِّلْمُتَّقِينَ ﴿٢﴾ الَّذِينَ يُؤْمِنُونَ بِالْغَيْبِ وَيُقِيمُونَ الصَّلَاةَ وَمِمَّا رَزَقْنَاهُمْ يُنفِقُونَ ﴿٣﴾ وَالَّذِينَ يُؤْمِنُونَ بِمَا أُنزِلَ إِلَيْكَ وَمَا أُنزِلَ مِن قَبْلِكَ وَبِالْآخِرَةِ هُمْ يُوقِنُونَ ﴿٤﴾ أُولَٰئِكَ عَلَىٰ هُدًى مِّن رَّبِّهِمْ ۖ وَأُولَٰئِكَ هُمُ الْمُفْلِحُونَ ﴿٥﴾ [البقرة: 1-5]

Alif, Lam, Meem. (1) This is the Book about which there is no doubt, a guidance for those conscious of Allah - (2) Who believe in the unseen, establish prayer, and spend out of what We have provided for them, (3) And who believe in what has been revealed to you, [O Muhammad], and what was revealed before you, and of the Hereafter they are certain [in faith]. (4) Those are upon [right] guidance from their Lord, and it is those who are the successful. (5)

Aliflammeem (1) Thalika alkitabu la rayba feehi hudan lilmuttaqeena (2) Allatheena yuminoona bialghaybi wayuqeemoona alssalata wamimma razaqnahum yunfiqoona (3) Waallatheena yuminoona bima onzila ilayka wama onzila min qablika wabialakhirati hum yooqinoona (4) Olaika AAala hudan min rabbihim waolaika humu almuflihoona (5)

اللَّهُ لَا إِلَٰهَ إِلَّا هُوَ الْحَيُّ الْقَيُّومُ ۚ لَا تَأْخُذُهُ سِنَةٌ وَلَا نَوْمٌ ۚ لَّهُ مَا فِي السَّمَاوَاتِ وَمَا فِي الْأَرْضِ ۗ مَن ذَا الَّذِي يَشْفَعُ عِندَهُ إِلَّا بِإِذْنِهِ ۚ يَعْلَمُ مَا بَيْنَ أَيْدِيهِمْ وَمَا خَلْفَهُمْ ۖ وَلَا يُحِيطُونَ بِشَيْءٍ مِّنْ عِلْمِهِ إِلَّا بِمَا شَاءَ ۚ وَسِعَ كُرْسِيُّهُ السَّمَاوَاتِ وَالْأَرْضَ ۖ وَلَا يَئُودُهُ حِفْظُهُمَا ۚ وَهُوَ الْعَلِيُّ الْعَظِيمُ ﴿٢٥٥﴾ لَا إِكْرَاهَ فِي الدِّينِ ۖ قَد تَّبَيَّنَ الرُّشْدُ مِنَ الْغَيِّ ۚ فَمَن يَكْفُرْ بِالطَّاغُوتِ وَيُؤْمِن بِاللَّهِ فَقَدِ اسْتَمْسَكَ بِالْعُرْوَةِ الْوُثْقَىٰ لَا انفِصَامَ لَهَا ۗ وَاللَّهُ سَمِيعٌ عَلِيمٌ ﴿٢٥٦﴾ اللَّهُ وَلِيُّ الَّذِينَ آمَنُوا يُخْرِجُهُم مِّنَ الظُّلُمَاتِ إِلَى النُّورِ ۖ وَالَّذِينَ كَفَرُوا أَوْلِيَاؤُهُمُ الطَّاغُوتُ يُخْرِجُونَهُم مِّنَ النُّورِ إِلَى الظُّلُمَاتِ ۗ أُولَٰئِكَ أَصْحَابُ النَّارِ ۖ هُمْ فِيهَا خَالِدُونَ ﴿٢٥٧﴾ أَلَمْ تَرَ إِلَى الَّذِي حَاجَّ إِبْرَاهِيمَ فِي رَبِّهِ أَنْ آتَاهُ اللَّهُ الْمُلْكَ إِذْ قَالَ إِبْرَاهِيمُ رَبِّيَ الَّذِي يُحْيِي وَيُمِيتُ قَالَ أَنَا أُحْيِي وَأُمِيتُ ۖ قَالَ إِبْرَاهِيمُ فَإِنَّ اللَّهَ يَأْتِي بِالشَّمْسِ مِنَ الْمَشْرِقِ فَأْتِ بِهَا مِنَ الْمَغْرِبِ فَبُهِتَ الَّذِي كَفَرَ ۗ وَاللَّهُ لَا يَهْدِي الْقَوْمَ الظَّالِمِينَ ﴿٢٥٨﴾ [البقرة: ٢٥٥-٢٥٨]

Allahu la ilaha illa huwa alhayyu alqayyoomu la takhuthuhu sinatun wala nawmun lahu ma fee alssamawati wama fee alardi man tha allathee yashfaAAu AAindahu illa biithnihi yaAAlamu ma bayna aydeehim wama khalfahum wala yuheetoona bishayin min AAilmihi illa bima shaa wasiAAa kursiyyuhu alssamawati waalarda wala yaooduhu hifthuhuma wahuwa alAAaliyyu alAAatheemu (255) La ikraha fee alddeeni qad tabayyana alrrushdu mina alghayyi faman yakfur bialttaghooti wayumin biAllahi faqadi istamsaka bialAAurwati alwuthqa la infisama laha waAllahu sameeAAun AAaleemun (256) Allahu waliyyu allatheena amanoo yukhrijuhum mina alththulumati ila alnnoori waallatheena kafaroo awliyaohumu alttaghootu yukhrijoonahum mina alnnoori ila alththulumati olaika ashabu alnnari hum feeha khalidoona (257) Alam tara ila allathee hajja ibraheema fee rabbihi an atahu Allahu almulka ith qala ibraheemu rabbiya allathee yuhyee wayumeetu qala ana ohyee waomeetu qala ibraheemu fainna Allaha yatee bialshshamsi mina almashriqi fati biha mina almaghribi fabuhita allathee kafara waAllahu la yahdee alqawma alththalimeena (258)

Allah - there is no deity except Him, the Ever-Living, the Sustainer of [all] existence. Neither drowsiness overtakes Him nor sleep. To Him belongs whatever is in the heavens and whatever is on the earth. Who is it that can intercede with Him except by His permission? He knows what is [presently] before them and what will be after them, and they encompass not a thing of His knowledge except for what He wills. His Kursi extends over the heavens and the earth, and their preservation tires Him not. And He is the Most High, the Most Great. (255) There shall be no compulsion in [acceptance of] the religion. The right course has become clear from the wrong. So whoever disbelieves in Taghut and believes in Allah has grasped the most trustworthy handhold with no break in it. And Allah is Hearing and Knowing. (256) Allah is the ally of those who believe. He brings them out from darknesses into the light. And those who disbelieve - their allies are Taghut. They take them out of the light into darknesses. Those are the companions of the Fire; they will abide eternally therein. (257) Have you not considered the one who argued with Abraham about his Lord [merely] because Allah had given him kingship? When Abraham said, "My Lord is the one who gives life and causes death," he said, "I give life and cause death." Abraham said, "Indeed, Allah brings up the sun from the east, so bring it up from the west." So the disbeliever was overwhelmed [by astonishment], and Allah does not guide the wrongdoing people. (258)

آمَنَ الرَّسُولُ بِمَا أُنزِلَ إِلَيْهِ مِن رَّبِّهِ وَالْمُؤْمِنُونَ ۚ كُلٌّ آمَنَ بِاللَّهِ وَمَلَائِكَتِهِ وَكُتُبِهِ وَرُسُلِهِ لَا نُفَرِّقُ بَيْنَ أَحَدٍ مِّن رُّسُلِهِ ۚ وَقَالُوا سَمِعْنَا وَأَطَعْنَا ۖ غُفْرَانَكَ رَبَّنَا وَإِلَيْكَ الْمَصِيرُ

﴿٢٨٥﴾ لَا يُكَلِّفُ اللَّهُ نَفْسًا إِلَّا وُسْعَهَا ۚ لَهَا مَا كَسَبَتْ وَعَلَيْهَا مَا اكْتَسَبَتْ ۗ رَبَّنَا لَا تُؤَاخِذْنَا إِن نَّسِينَا أَوْ أَخْطَأْنَا ۚ رَبَّنَا وَلَا تَحْمِلْ عَلَيْنَا إِصْرًا كَمَا حَمَلْتَهُ عَلَى الَّذِينَ مِن قَبْلِنَا ۚ رَبَّنَا وَلَا تُحَمِّلْنَا مَا لَا طَاقَةَ لَنَا بِهِ ۖ وَاعْفُ عَنَّا وَاغْفِرْ لَنَا وَارْحَمْنَا ۚ أَنتَ مَوْلَانَا فَانصُرْنَا عَلَى الْقَوْمِ الْكَافِرِينَ ﴿٢٨٦﴾ [البقرة: 285- 286]

Amana alrrasoolu bima onzila ilayhi min rabbihi waalmuminoona kullun amana biAllahi wamalaikatihi wakutubihi warusulihi la nufarriqu bayna ahadin min rusulihi waqaloo samiAAna waataAAna ghufranaka rabbana wailayka almaseeru (285) La yukallifu Allahu nafsan illa wusAAaha laha ma kasabat waAAalayha ma iktasabat rabbana la tuakhithna in naseena aw akhtana rabbana wala tahmil AAalayna isran kama hamaltahu AAala allatheena min qablina rabbana wala tuhammilna ma la taqata lana bihi waoAAfu AAanna waighfir lana wairhamna anta mawlana faonsurna AAala alqawmi alkafireena (286)

148

The Messenger has believed in what was revealed to him from
his Lord, and [so have] the believers. All of them have believed
in Allah and His angels and His books and His messengers,
[saying], "We make no distinction between any of His
messengers." And they say, "We hear and we obey. [We seek]
Your forgiveness, our Lord, and to You is the [final]
destination." (285) Allah does not charge a soul except [with
that within] its capacity. It will have [the consequence of] what
[good] it has gained, and it will bear [the consequence of] what
[evil] it has earned. "Our Lord, do not impose blame upon us if
we have forgotten or erred. Our Lord, and lay not upon us a
burden like that which You laid upon those before us. Our Lord,
and burden us not with that which we have no ability to bear.
And pardon us; and forgive us; and have mercy upon us. You
are our protector, so give us victory over the disbelieving
people." (286)

وَاتَّبَعُوا مَا تَتْلُو الشَّيَاطِينُ عَلَىٰ مُلْكِ سُلَيْمَانَ ۖ وَمَا كَفَرَ سُلَيْمَانُ وَلَٰكِنَّ
الشَّيَاطِينَ كَفَرُوا يُعَلِّمُونَ النَّاسَ السِّحْرَ وَمَا أُنزِلَ عَلَى الْمَلَكَيْنِ بِبَابِلَ هَارُوتَ
وَمَارُوتَ ۚ وَمَا يُعَلِّمَانِ مِنْ أَحَدٍ حَتَّىٰ يَقُولَا إِنَّمَا نَحْنُ فِتْنَةٌ فَلَا تَكْفُرْ ۖ فَيَتَعَلَّمُونَ
مِنْهُمَا مَا يُفَرِّقُونَ بِهِ بَيْنَ الْمَرْءِ وَزَوْجِهِ ۚ وَمَا هُم بِضَارِّينَ بِهِ مِنْ أَحَدٍ إِلَّا بِإِذْنِ اللَّهِ ۚ
وَيَتَعَلَّمُونَ مَا يَضُرُّهُمْ وَلَا يَنفَعُهُمْ ۚ وَلَقَدْ عَلِمُوا لَمَنِ اشْتَرَاهُ مَا لَهُ فِي الْآخِرَةِ مِنْ
خَلَاقٍ ۚ وَلَبِئْسَ مَا شَرَوْا بِهِ أَنفُسَهُمْ ۚ لَوْ كَانُوا يَعْلَمُونَ ﴿١٠٢﴾ [البقرة: 102]

WaittabaAAoo ma tatloo alshshayateenu AAala mulki sulaymana
wama kafara sulaymanu walakinna alshshayateena kafaroo
yuAAallimoona alnnasa alssihra wama onzila AAala almalakayni
bibabila haroota wamaroota wama yuAAallimani min ahadin
hatta yaqoola innama nahnu fitnatun fala takfur
fayataAAallamoona minhuma ma yufarriqoona bihi bayna almari
wazawjihi wama hum bidarreena bihi min ahadin illa biithni
Allahi wayataAAallamoona ma yadurruhum wala yanfaAAuhum
walaqad AAalimoo lamani ishtarahu ma lahu fee alakhirati min
khalaqin walabisa ma sharaw bihi anfusahum law kanoo
yaAAlamoona (102)

And they followed [instead] what the devils had recited during the reign of Solomon. It was not Solomon who disbelieved, but the devils disbelieved, teaching people magic and that which was revealed to the two angels at Babylon, Harut and Marut. But the two angels do not teach anyone unless they say, "We are a trial, so do not disbelieve [by practicing magic]." And [yet] they learn from them that by which they cause separation between a man and his wife. But they do not harm anyone through it except by permission of Allah. And the people learn what harms them and does not benefit them. But the Children of Israel certainly knew that whoever purchased the magic would not have in the Hereafter any share. And wretched is that for which they sold themselves, if they only knew. (102)

﴿ وَأَوْحَيْنَا إِلَى مُوسَىٰ أَنْ أَلْقِ عَصَاكَ ۖ فَإِذَا هِيَ تَلْقَفُ مَا يَأْفِكُونَ ﴿١١٧﴾ فَوَقَعَ الْحَقُّ وَبَطَلَ مَا كَانُوا يَعْمَلُونَ ﴿١١٨﴾ فَغُلِبُوا هُنَالِكَ وَانقَلَبُوا صَاغِرِينَ ﴿١١٩﴾ وَأُلْقِيَ السَّحَرَةُ سَاجِدِينَ ﴿١٢٠﴾ قَالُوا آمَنَّا بِرَبِّ الْعَالَمِينَ ﴿١٢١﴾ رَبِّ مُوسَىٰ وَهَارُونَ ﴿١٢٢﴾

[الأعراف: 117-122]

Waawhayna ila moosa an alqi AAasaka faitha hiya talqafu ma yafikoona (117) FawaqaAAa alhaqqu wabatala ma kanoo yaAAmaloona (118) Faghuliboo hunalika wainqalaboo saghireena (119) Waolqiya alssaharatu sajideena (120) Qaloo amanna birabbi alAAalameena (121) Rabbi moosa waharoona (122)

And We inspired to Moses, "Throw your staff," and at once it devoured what they were falsifying. (117) So the truth was established, and abolished was what they were doing. (118) And Pharaoh and his people were overcome right there and became debased. (119) And the magicians fell down in prostration [to Allah]. (120) They said, "We have believed in the Lord of the worlds, (121) The Lord of Moses and Aaron." (122)

وَقَالَ فِرْعَوْنُ ائْتُونِي بِكُلِّ سَاحِرٍ عَلِيمٍ ﴿٧٩﴾ فَلَمَّا جَاءَ السَّحَرَةُ قَالَ لَهُم مُّوسَىٰ أَلْقُوا مَا أَنتُم مُّلْقُونَ ﴿٨٠﴾ فَلَمَّا أَلْقَوْا قَالَ مُوسَىٰ مَا جِئْتُم بِهِ السِّحْرُ إِنَّ اللَّهَ سَيُبْطِلُهُ إِنَّ اللَّهَ لَا يُصْلِحُ عَمَلَ الْمُفْسِدِينَ ﴿٨١﴾ [يونس: 79-81]

Waqala firAAawnu itoonee bikulli sahirin AAaleemin
alqoo ma jaa alssaharatu qala lahum moosa Falamma (79)
jitum bihi ma alqaw qala moosa Falamma (80) antum mulqoona
yuslihu AAamala alssihru inna Allaha sayubtiluhu inna Allaha la
(81) almufsideena

And Pharaoh said, "Bring to me every learned magician." (79) So
when the magicians came, Moses said to them, "Throw down
whatever you will throw." (80) And when they had thrown, Moses
said, "What you have brought is [only] magic. Indeed, Allah will
expose its worthlessness. Indeed, Allah does not amend the work of
corrupters. (81)

قَالُوا يَا مُوسَىٰ إِمَّا أَن تُلْقِيَ وَإِمَّا أَن نَّكُونَ أَوَّلَ مَنْ أَلْقَىٰ ﴿٦٥﴾ قَالَ بَلْ أَلْقُوا فَإِذَا حِبَالُهُمْ وَعِصِيُّهُمْ يُخَيَّلُ إِلَيْهِ مِن سِحْرِهِمْ أَنَّهَا تَسْعَىٰ ﴿٦٦﴾ فَأَوْجَسَ فِي نَفْسِهِ خِيفَةً مُّوسَىٰ ﴿٦٧﴾ قُلْنَا لَا تَخَفْ إِنَّكَ أَنتَ الْأَعْلَىٰ ﴿٦٨﴾ وَأَلْقِ مَا فِي يَمِينِكَ تَلْقَفْ مَا صَنَعُوا إِنَّمَا صَنَعُوا كَيْدُ سَاحِرٍ وَلَا يُفْلِحُ السَّاحِرُ حَيْثُ أَتَىٰ ﴿٦٩﴾

[طه: 65-69]

Qaloo ya moosa imma an tulqiya waimma an nakoona awwala
man alqa (65) Qala bal alqoo faitha hibaluhum waAAisiyyuhum
yukhayyalu ilayhi min sihrihim annaha tasAAa (66) Faawjasa fee
nafsihi kheefatan moosa (67) Qulna la takhaf innaka anta alaAAla
(68) Waalqi ma fee yameenika talqaf ma sanaAAoo innama
sanaAAoo kaydu sahirin wala yuflihu alssahiru haythu ata (69)

They said, "O Moses, either you throw or we will be the first to
throw." (65) He said, "Rather, you throw." And suddenly their

151

ropes and staffs seemed to him from their magic that they were moving [like snakes]. (66)   And he sensed within himself apprehension, did Moses. (67)   Allah said, "Fear not. Indeed, it is you who are superior. (68)   And throw what is in your right hand; it will swallow up what they have crafted. What they have crafted is but the trick of a magician, and the magician will not succeed wherever he is." (69)

وَإِذْ يَعِدُكُمُ اللَّهُ إِحْدَى الطَّائِفَتَيْنِ أَنَّهَا لَكُمْ وَتَوَدُّونَ أَنَّ غَيْرَ ذَاتِ الشَّوْكَةِ تَكُونُ لَكُمْ وَيُرِيدُ اللَّهُ أَن يُحِقَّ الْحَقَّ بِكَلِمَاتِهِ وَيَقْطَعَ دَابِرَ الْكَافِرِينَ ﴿٧﴾ لِيُحِقَّ الْحَقَّ وَيُبْطِلَ الْبَاطِلَ وَلَوْ كَرِهَ الْمُجْرِمُونَ ﴿٨﴾ [الأنفال: 7-8]

Waith yaAAidukumu Allahu ihda alttaifatayni annaha lakum watawaddoona anna ghayra thati alshshawkati takoonu lakum wayureedu Allahu an yuhiqqa alhaqqa bikalimatihi wayaqtaAAa dabira alkafireena (7)   Liyuhiqqa alhaqqa wayubtila albatila walaw kariha almujrimoona (8)

[Remember, O believers], when Allah promised you one of the two groups - that it would be yours - and you wished that the unarmed one would be yours. But Allah intended to establish the truth by His words and to eliminate the disbelievers (7)   That He should establish the truth and abolish falsehood, even if the criminals disliked it. (8)

﴿٢٣﴾ وَقَدِمْنَا إِلَى مَا عَمِلُوا مِنْ عَمَلٍ فَجَعَلْنَاهُ هَبَاءً مَّنثُورًا [الفرقان: 23]

Waqadimna ila ma AAamiloo min AAamalin fajaAAalnahu habaan manthooran (23)

And We will regard what they have done of deeds and make them as dust dispersed. (23)

152

قُلْ إِنَّ رَبِّي يَقْذِفُ بِالْحَقِّ عَلَّامُ الْغُيُوبِ ﴿٤٨﴾ قُلْ جَاءَ الْحَقُّ وَمَا يُبْدِئُ الْبَاطِلُ وَمَا يُعِيدُ ﴿٤٩﴾ [سبأ: 48-49]

Qul inna rabbee yaqthifu bialhaqqi AAallamu alghuyoobi (48) Qul jaa alhaqqu wama yubdio albatilu wama yuAAeedu (49)

Say, "Indeed, my Lord projects the truth. Knower of the unseen." (48) Say, "The truth has come, and falsehood can neither begin [anything] nor repeat [it]." (49)

وَقُلْ جَاءَ الْحَقُّ وَزَهَقَ الْبَاطِلُ ۚ إِنَّ الْبَاطِلَ كَانَ زَهُوقًا ﴿٨١﴾ [الأسراء: 81]

Waqul jaa alhaqqu wazahaqa albatilu inna albatila kana zahooqan (81)

And say, "Truth has come, and falsehood has departed. Indeed is falsehood, [by nature], ever bound to depart." (81)

بَلْ نَقْذِفُ بِالْحَقِّ عَلَى الْبَاطِلِ فَيَدْمَغُهُ فَإِذَا هُوَ زَاهِقٌ ۚ وَلَكُمُ الْوَيْلُ مِمَّا تَصِفُونَ ﴿١٨﴾ [الأنبياء: 18]

huwa albatili fayadmaghuhu faitha Bal naqthifu bialhaqqi AAala (18) tasifoona zahiqun walakumu alwaylu mimma

Rather, We dash the truth upon falsehood, and it destroys it, and thereupon it departs. And for you is destruction from that which you describe. (18)

قَاتِلُوهُمْ يُعَذِّبْهُمُ اللَّهُ بِأَيْدِيكُمْ وَيُخْزِهِمْ وَيَنْصُرْكُمْ عَلَيْهِمْ وَيَشْفِ صُدُورَ قَوْمٍ مُؤْمِنِينَ ﴿١٤﴾ وَيُذْهِبْ غَيْظَ قُلُوبِهِمْ ۗ وَيَتُوبُ اللَّهُ عَلَى مَن يَشَاءُ ۗ وَاللَّهُ عَلِيمٌ حَكِيمٌ ﴿١٥﴾ [التوبة: 14-15]

153

Qatiloohum yuAAaththibhumu Allahu biaydeekum wayukhzihim
wayansurkum AAalayhim wayashfi sudoora qawmin mumineena
(14) Wayuthhib ghaytha quloobihim wayatoobu Allahu AAala
man yashao waAllahu AAaleemun hakeemun (15)

Fight them; Allah will punish them by your hands and will disgrace
them and give you victory over them and satisfy the breasts of a
believing people (14)   And remove the fury in the believers' hearts.
And Allah turns in forgiveness to whom He wills; and Allah is
Knowing and Wise. (15)

يَا أَيُّهَا النَّاسُ قَدْ جَاءَتْكُم مَّوْعِظَةٌ مِّن رَّبِّكُمْ وَشِفَاءٌ لِّمَا فِي الصُّدُورِ وَهُدًى وَرَحْمَةٌ
لِّلْمُؤْمِنِينَ ﴿٥٧﴾ [يونس: 57]

Ya ayyuha alnnasu qad jaatkum mawAAithatun min rabbikum
washifaon lima fee alssudoori wahudan warahmatun lilmumineena
(57)

O mankind, there has to come to you instruction from your Lord
and healing for what is in the breasts and guidance and mercy for
the believers. (57)

وَأَوْحَىٰ رَبُّكَ إِلَى النَّحْلِ أَنِ اتَّخِذِي مِنَ الْجِبَالِ بُيُوتًا وَمِنَ الشَّجَرِ وَمِمَّا يَعْرِشُونَ
﴿٦٨﴾ ثُمَّ كُلِي مِن كُلِّ الثَّمَرَاتِ فَاسْلُكِي سُبُلَ رَبِّكِ ذُلُلًا ۚ يَخْرُجُ مِن بُطُونِهَا
شَرَابٌ مُّخْتَلِفٌ أَلْوَانُهُ فِيهِ شِفَاءٌ لِّلنَّاسِ ۗ إِنَّ فِي ذَٰلِكَ لَآيَةً لِّقَوْمٍ يَتَفَكَّرُونَ
﴿٦٩﴾ [النحل: 68-69]

Waawha rabbuka ila alnnahli ani ittakhithee mina aljibali
buyootan wamina alshshajari wamimma yaAArishoona
(68)   Thumma kulee min kulli aththamarati faoslukee subula
rabbiki thululan yakhruju min butooniha sharabun mukhtalifun
alwanuhu feehi shifaon lilnnasi inna fee thalika laayatan liqawmin
yatafakkaroona (69)

And your Lord inspired to the bee, "Take for yourself among the
mountains, houses, and among the trees and [in] that which they

154

construct. (68) Then eat from all the fruits and follow the ways of your Lord laid down [for you]." There emerges from their bellies a drink, varying in colors, in which there is healing for people. Indeed in that is a sign for a people who give thought. (69)

وَنُنَزِّلُ مِنَ الْقُرْآنِ مَا هُوَ شِفَاءٌ وَرَحْمَةٌ لِّلْمُؤْمِنِينَ ۙ وَلَا يَزِيدُ الظَّالِمِينَ إِلَّا خَسَارًا ﴿٨٢﴾ [الإسراء: 82]

Wanunazzilu mina alqurani ma huwa shifaon warahmatun lilmumineena wala yazeedu alththalimeena illa khasaran (82)

And We send down of the Qur'an that which is healing and mercy for the believers, but it does not increase the wrongdoers except in loss. (82)

وَإِذَا مَرِضْتُ فَهُوَ يَشْفِينِ ﴿٨٠﴾ [الشعراء: 80]

Waitha maridtu fahuwa yashfeeni (80)

And when I am ill, it is He who cures me (80)

وَلَوْ جَعَلْنَاهُ قُرْآنًا أَعْجَمِيًّا لَّقَالُوا لَوْلَا فُصِّلَتْ آيَاتُهُ ۖ أَأَعْجَمِيٌّ وَعَرَبِيٌّ ۗ قُلْ هُوَ لِلَّذِينَ آمَنُوا هُدًى وَشِفَاءٌ ۖ وَالَّذِينَ لَا يُؤْمِنُونَ فِي آذَانِهِمْ وَقْرٌ وَهُوَ عَلَيْهِمْ عَمًى ۚ أُولَٰئِكَ يُنَادَوْنَ مِن مَّكَانٍ بَعِيدٍ ﴿٤٤﴾ [فصلت: 44]

Walaw jaAAalnahu quranan aAAjamiyyan laqaloo lawla fussilat ayatuhu aAAjamiyyun waAAarabiyyun qul huwa lillatheena amanoo hudan washifaon waallatheena la yuminoona fee athanihim waqrun wahuwa AAalayhim AAaman olaika yunadawna min makanin baAAeedin (44)

And if We had made it a non-Arabic Qur'an, they would have said, "Why are its verses not explained in detail [in our language]? Is it a foreign [recitation] and an Arab [messenger]?" Say, "It is, for those who believe, a guidance and cure." And those who do not believe - in their ears is deafness, and it is upon them blindness. Those are being called from a distant place. (44)

بِسْمِ اللَّهِ الرَّحْمَٰنِ الرَّحِيمِ

Bismi Allahi alrrahmani alrraheem

In the name of Allah , the Entirely Merciful, the Especially Merciful

قُلْ هُوَ اللَّهُ أَحَدٌ ﴿١﴾ اللَّهُ الصَّمَدُ ﴿٢﴾ لَمْ يَلِدْ وَلَمْ يُولَدْ ﴿٣﴾ وَلَمْ يَكُن لَّهُ كُفُوًا أَحَدٌ ﴿٤﴾ [الإخلاص: 1-4]

Qul huwa Allahu ahadun (1) Allahu alssamadu (2) Lam yalid walam yooladu (3) Walam yakun lahu kufuwan ahadun (4)

Say, "He is Allah, [who is] One, (1) Allah, the Eternal Refuge. (2) He neither begets nor is born, (3) Nor is there to Him any equivalent." (4)

بِسْمِ اللَّهِ الرَّحْمَٰنِ الرَّحِيمِ

Bismi Allahi alrrahmani alrraheemi

In the name of Allah, the Entirely Merciful, the Especially Merciful

قُلْ أَعُوذُ بِرَبِّ الْفَلَقِ ﴿١﴾ مِن شَرِّ مَا خَلَقَ ﴿٢﴾ وَمِن شَرِّ غَاسِقٍ إِذَا وَقَبَ ﴿٣﴾ وَمِن شَرِّ النَّفَّاثَاتِ فِي الْعُقَدِ ﴿٤﴾ وَمِن شَرِّ حَاسِدٍ إِذَا حَسَدَ ﴿٥﴾[الفلق: 1-5]

Qul aAAoothu birabbi alfalaqi (1) Min sharri ma khalaqa (2) Wamin sharri ghasiqin itha waqaba (3) Wamin sharri

alnnaffathati fee alAAuqadi (4) Wamin sharri hasidin itha hasada
(5)

Say, "I seek refuge in the Lord of daybreak (1) From the evil of
that which He created (2) And from the evil of darkness when it
settles (3) And from the evil of the blowers in knots (4) And from
the evil of an envier when he envies." (5)

بِسْمِ اللَّهِ الرَّحْمَٰنِ الرَّحِيمِ

Bismi Allahi alrrahmani alrraheemi

In the name of Allah, the Entirely Merciful, the Especially Merciful

قُلْ أَعُوذُ بِرَبِّ النَّاسِ ﴿١﴾ مَلِكِ النَّاسِ ﴿٢﴾ إِلَٰهِ النَّاسِ ﴿٣﴾ مِن شَرِّ
الْوَسْوَاسِ الْخَنَّاسِ ﴿٤﴾ الَّذِي يُوَسْوِسُ فِي صُدُورِ النَّاسِ ﴿٥﴾ مِنَ الْجِنَّةِ
وَالنَّاسِ ﴿٦﴾ [الناس: 1-5]

Qul aAAoothu birabbi alnnasi (1) Maliki alnnasi (2) Ilahi alnnasi
(3) Min sharri alwaswasi alkhannasi (4) Allathee yuwaswisu fee
sudoori alnnasi (5) Mina aljinnati wa alnnasm (6)

Say, "I seek refuge in the Lord of mankind, (1) The Sovereign of
mankind. (2) The God of mankind, (3) From the evil of the
retreating whisperer - (4) Who whispers [evil] into the breasts of
mankind - (5) From among the Jinn and mankind." (6)

Conclusion

I pray to Allah that you have benefitted from this handbook. I have tried my best to keep this book to the Qur'an and Sunnah, and summarised for ease of reading for the reader.

In this handbook, I have tried to address the ethical concepts of Ruqya and its guidelines by the Ahl al-Sunnah wal-Jama'ah which I believe is indispensable for Muslims and non-Muslims alike.

All the information that I have chosen to put this in book are much more valuable and beneficial when put into practice with perseverance. Every topic touched upon in this handbook is derived from the Qur'anic verses, the Prophetic traditions, and the scholars from the past and present.

All success is from Allah. May this handbook bring benefit, mercy, and blessings to every reader. Ameen.

For more information on the topic, please visit www.ruqyainlondon.com.

About the Author

Raqi Abu Nadeer has been performing Ruqya over 20 years, treating and counseling people with various spiritual afflictions by the permission of Allah. He is a highly experienced and competent Raqi who is recognized by the scholars in the field of Ruqya.

Currently, Raqi Abu Nadeer runs Alruqya Healing clinic in London which is the subsidiary of Ruqya International Academy run by Sheikh Khalid Al-Hibshi who is a prominent leading scholar from Saudi Arabia specializing in the field of Ruqya treatment for evil eye, black magic, and Jinn possession. Sheikh Khalid has been certified by leading scholars to teach the subject of Ruqya and to perform Ruqya. Sheikh Khalid has been performing Ruqya for over 30 years.

Raqi Abu Nadeer's expertise, knowledge and dedication in the sciences of Ruqya and benefiting others also leads him to deliver regular educational workshops, training and courses to patients, practitioners/therapists as well as to organizations with the primary focus on how to better understand and effectively deal with the different aspects of spiritual affliction in the light of the Qur'an and Sunnah.

Printed in Great Britain
by Amazon

61976950R00104